FROM DOGS TO DISCIPLES

From Dogs to Disciples

Matthew's Message of Inclusion for Outcasts

Nathan Peeler

To Hayley

My companion and helper (Prov 18.22).

And Matthias and Malachi

Whose births gave me a glimpse of the Heavenly Father's love for us.
May you come to know His love, follow Him,
and be fishers of men (Matt 4.19).

CONTENTS

I

INTRODUCTION

A causal reading of the Jewish Scriptures might give the impression that Yahweh was simply concerned about his relationship with the Jewish nation. Upon a closer reading, an abundance of evidence shows that Yahweh welcomes any who comes to him: Melchizedek, Rahab, Naaman, and even Nebuchadnezzar. At first glance, the gospel of Matthew appears to be written by a Jew to a Jewish audience and one would expect overly Jewish themes. However, when the gospel is read carefully, one sees that Jesus mirrors the example of Yahweh and accepts any who come to him. Jesus is so radical that not only does he welcome all but accepts those which many in society would consider outcasts.

Jesus was a Jew, born to a Jewish family (Matt 1.1), who carefully observed the Law of Moses.[1] Joseph, Jesus' supposed earthly father, was a righteous man (Matt. 1.18) and Mary was highly favored of the Lord (Luke. 1.28, 45, 48). Jesus was circumcised on the eighth day (Luke. 2.21) and Mary offered the purification sacrifice required in the Law of Moses (Luke. 2.22–24). From a young age, many were impressed with Jesus' understanding and questions concerning the Holy Scriptures (Luke. 2.46–47).[2] Jesus

---

[1] Bruce L. Shelley, *Church History in Plain Language*, 4th Edition, Revised by R. L. Hatchett (Nashville: Thomas Nelson, 2013), 3.

[2] Of course, the Holy Scriptures of Jesus day would be what modern Christians call the Old Testament.

and His disciples worshiped at the local synagogues (12.9; 13.54; see also Luke. 4.16) where the Law of Moses and the prophets were read every Sabbath (Acts 13.15, 27; 15.21).

After beginning His public ministry, Jesus selected twelve Jewish men to be His disciples. The number of disciples was intentionally symbolic of the tribes of Israel (19.28).[3] In fact, Matthew presents Jesus as having experiences similar to those of the nation of Israel. He fled to Egypt, was called out of Egypt, was tempted in the wilderness for 40 days, and spent time by the Jordan River. Indeed, Jesus and His disciples had a very Jewish experience.

Most scholars accept that Matthew was a Jew writing to a largely Jewish audience[4] with a date ranging from AD 55–80.[5] Matthew's gospel begins in a very Jewish way: a genealogy. The Jews placed great importance in their lineage (1 Chron 1–9; Ezra 2.62; Neh. 7.64; Matt 3.9; Luke 2.36; 3.8; John 8.39; Acts

---

[3] R. T. France, *The Gospel of Matthew*, The New International Commentary of the New Testament (Grand Rapids: William B. Eerdmans Publishing Company, 2007), 376.

[4] France, *The Gospel of Matthew*, 15–16. There are some scholars who deviate from this such as David Garland, *Reading Matthew: A Literary and Theological Commentary* (Macon, GA: Smyth & Helwys Publishing, Inc., 2001), 2–3. Garland cites "anti-Jewish bias" and passages of inclusion of Gentiles to argue Matthew wrote to a group of Christians that was equally Jew and Gentile. Others have stated the book is anti-Jewish and the readers were Gentiles. The religious leaders are almost always depicted negatively and seeking to murder Jesus. Matthew is the only gospel that records the statement, "His blood shall be on us and on our children" (27.25). For a good, brief rundown of those who argue for Gentile authorship see R. T. France, *Matthew: Evangelist and Teacher* (Downers Grove: InterVarsity Press, 1989), 102–108.

[5] For our purposes the date is not that big of an issue. Either way the book is dated, the early church would have still faced the same obstacles of accepting Gentiles and women. For good, but brief, arguments for the early and late date of Matthew see D.A. Carson, Douglas J. Moo, and Leon Morris, *An Introduction to the New Testament* (Grand Rapids: Zondervan, 1992), 76–79.

26.7; Phil 3.5). What better way to begin a gospel written to a Jewish audience than to show Jesus' descent from two central Jewish characters, Abraham and David? God made amazing promises to these two men, promises replete with nationalistic implications. Matthew used the Jewish title "Son of David" more than the rest of the New Testament combined. Matthew utilizes this phrase nine times (1.1; 9.27; 12.23; 15.22; 20.30–31; 21.9, 15; 22.41–45), Mark three times (Mark. 10.47–48; 12.35), Luke twice (Luke 18.38–39), and it does not appear in the rest of the New Testament.[6] According to the Jewish Scriptures, the Messiah was intended to come through the line of David, and Matthew's use of this phrase depicts Jesus as fulfilling the Jewish expectation for the Messiah. Matthew emphasizes Jesus fulfilling the Scriptures more than any other gospel, a fitting theme if writing to a people steeped in the Jewish Scriptures and actively looking for the Messiah.

Evidence that the Jews are Matthew's targeted audience is abundant. Matthew emphasizes Jesus' mission to the Jews (10.5–6; 15.24) and feels no need to explain the Jewish custom of handwashing, whereas Mark does (compare Matt 15.1 with Mark 7.3). Only Matthew includes a defense of the temple tax (17.24–27), a custom familiar to Jewish readers. Furthermore, the author speaks about the seat of Moses (23.2), phylacteries and tassels (23.5), and other Jewish rituals which he assumes his audience understands. Additionally, Matthew's use of the phrase "kingdom of heaven" has strong Jewish overtones. Matthew uses the phrase thirty-three times, but the phrase is not employed by any other New Testament writer. In parallel passages, Mark and Luke use the phrase "kingdom of God."[7]

---

[6] The closest references would be Rom 1.3; 2 Tim 2.8, which both use "descendant of David" rather than "Son of David." There is also the use of "root of David" in Rev 5.5; 22.16.

[7] Craig L. Blomberg, *Jesus and the Gospels: An Introduction and Survey* (Nashville: Broadman & Holman Publishers, 1997), 131.

Contrary to modern scholars, who argue Mark was written first, the early church fathers unanimously testify that Matthew was the first gospel written. They claim it was written by the apostle Matthew, the tax collector turned disciple, to Jews who recognized Jesus as the Messiah. Two examples will suffice. Around AD 180, Pantaenus[8] traveled to India and discovered that Bartholomew, one of the apostles, had previously evangelized the area and left behind "Matthew's account in Hebrew letters..."[9] Origen wrote, "I have learned by tradition the Gospel according to Matthew...was written first and that he composed it in the Hebrew tongue and published it for the converts from Judaism."[10]

---

[8] Pantaenus (AD 120–216) was a highly educated Stoic philosopher and distinguished preacher. He ran the School of Alexandria for several years before embarking on missionary work.

[9] Eusebius, *Ecclesiastical History*, 5.10.3.

[10] Eusebius 6.25.4. For the reader interested in investigating this issue further here is a little more information:

Eusebius includes Matthew in undisputed books of the New Testament and writes: "Matthew at first preached to Hebrews, and when he planned to go to others also, he wrote his gospel in his own native language for those he was leaving, his writing filling the gap left by his departure" (Eusebius, *Ecclesiastical History*, 3.24.6).

Papias lived-in modern-day Turkey, was a church leader, and wrote *Expositions of the Oracles of the Lord* around AD 130. Sadly, the document no longer exists but parts of it were copied by Eusebius, the father of church history. "So then Matthew wrote the oracles in the Hebrew language, and everyone interpreted them as he was able" (Eusebius, 3.39.16).

Origen (AD 185–254) wrote a commentary on the gospel of Matthew in which he writes, "Among the four gospels, which are the only indisputable ones in the Church of God under heaven, I have learned by tradition that the first was written by Matthew, who was once a tax collector, but afterwards an apostle of Jesus Christ, and it was prepared for the converts from Judaism, and published in the Hebrew language" (Eusebius 6.25.4).

Irenaeus, *Against Heresies* 3.1.1: Matthew also issued a written gospel among the Hebrews in their own dialect..."

Epiphanius *Panarion* 51.5.3: "Matthew himself wrote and issued the gospel in the Hebrew alphabet..."

Considering Jesus' Jewish background, strong grounding in the Jewish Scriptures, and His selection of an all-male following, one might read Matthew expecting to find a gospel message that primarily targets Jewish men. Given the poor social status of Gentiles and women during this time, this would not be surprising. However, upon closer scrutiny of Matthew's gospel, this could not be further from the truth. Matthew abounds with messages welcoming Gentiles and women into the fold of Christ! As the text is examined, the reader will witness the acceptance and approval of those who were typically rejected and distrusted. Not only will these "outsiders" be accepted, but they will be depicted as the ideal disciples in Matthew's gospel.

Augustine, *Harmony of the Gospels* 1.2.4: "Of these four, only Matthew is reckoned to have written in the Hebrew language…"

Jerome, *Lives of Illustrious Men* 3: "Matthew, also called Levi, apostle and aforetime publican, composed a gospel of Christ at first published in Judea in Hebrew for the sake of those of the circumcision who believed…"

II

BACKGROUND

Gentiles and Women in the First Century

Before plunging into an examination of the Gospel of Matthew and seeking to unearth the themes of inclusion of Gentiles and women, the time period must be briefly examined. Key questions that will aid in understanding the historical context of Matthew include: As best as can be understood, what relationship did Jews and Gentiles have in the First Century? What information does the New Testament give the reader about accepting Gentiles into the fold of God? What was life like for the average woman in this time period?

2.1 Jews and foreigners' relationship in First Century

The Jews' of the First Century had spent the better part of the last five centuries under foreign rule. From the time of Babylonian captivity in 586 BC to the Roman occupation depicted in the N.T., only once did the Jews briefly gain their independence during the Maccabean Revolt. Consequently, there is very little doubt that the Jews were heavily influenced by the Babylonians, Persians, Greeks, and Romans who occupied their homeland. In addition, "As many as two-thirds of the Jews in the First Century were living outside Palestine."[1] By the First Century, some Jews welcomed Hellenization while other Jews (namely,

---

[1] Everett Ferguson, *Backgrounds of Early Christianity*, 3rd Ed. (Grand Rapids: William B. Eerdmans Publishing Company, 2003), 427.

the Pharisees) fought against this process. Scholars debate what percentage of Jews fell into each group, but non-Jewish societies clearly impacted Jews.

2.1.1 Jew and Samaritan Relations

When Jesus spoke with the woman at the well in Samaria she was surprised and asked Jesus, "'How is it that You, being a Jew, ask me for a drink since I am a Samaritan woman?'" (John 4.9). John then adds the note, "For Jews have no dealings with Samaritans" (John 4.9). John, written many years after the other gospels,[2] explains some of the tensions which existed between the Jews and Samaritans. Later in John, the Jews want to insult Jesus so they accuse him of being a Samaritan and having a demon (John 8.48).

This tension has its roots in Assyrian captivity. In 722 BC Israel and some of Judah went into Assyrian captivity. Assyrian policy at that time was to mix nations they had defeated into a smorgasbord and place them in one area. This made it more difficult for a rebellion to take hold because people spoke different languages and practiced different customs. Since Jews were mixed in with other nations, the inevitable result was intermarriage, resulting in their children being half-Jew and half-pagan. These were to become known as Samaritans.

Differing beliefs between the Jews and Samaritans added fuel to the fire. It seems the Samaritans only accepted the Pentateuch as authoritative, but inserted some variant readings due to a difference of beliefs.[3] For example, following the Ten Commandments

---

[2] Eusebius 6.14.7. In this passage, Clement states that John was the last gospel written. See also Thomas D. Lea and David Alan Black, *The New Testament: Its Background and Message*, 2nd Ed. (Nashville: B&H Publishing Group, 2003), 158. For different arguments for dating the book of John, see D.A. Carson, Douglas J. Moo, and Leon Morris, *An Introduction to the New Testament*, 166–168.

[3] J. Julius Scott, Jr., *Jewish Backgrounds to the New Testament* (Grand Rapids: Baker Academic, 1995), 198 and Neil R. Lightfoot, *How We Got the Bible*, 3rd ed. (Grand Rapids: Baker Books, 2003), 142.

(Ex 20.1–17; Dt 5.6–21), the Samaritan Pentateuch inserts a long passage instructing Israel to build an altar on Mount Gerizim.[4] Around 150 BC, Josephus recorded an argument between Egyptian Jews and Samaritans before Ptolemy Philometor regarding the location of the true temple: Mount Gerizim or Mount Zion (*Ant.* 13.3.4).[5] Finally, around 108 BC John Hyrcanus, a Maccabean ruler, destroyed the Samaritan temple.[6]

While John 4 seems to indicate Jews kept their distance from the Samaritans, passages like Luke 9.51–56 show the Samaritans could be hostile toward the Jews as well. Jesus attempted to stay in a Samaritan village, but the town would not allow him to stay because He was going to Jerusalem (Luke 9.52–53). James and John are so angered by the actions of these Samaritans they request permission from Jesus to call down fire upon them (Luke 9.54), but Jesus rebukes them for their attitude and they travel to another village. Relations between Jews and Samaritans were very strained.

2.1.2 Jew–Gentile Relations
Passages like Luke 9.51–56 and John 4.9 imply a poor relationship between Jews and Samaritans, but what about other Gentiles? Most Greeks and Romans were hostile toward Jews.[7] Jews most likely reciprocated these feelings toward Greeks and Romans. Some centurions seemed to establish goodwill toward the Jewish community (Luke 7.4–5; Acts 10.1–2), but the presence

---

[4] Lightfoot, *How We Got the Bible*, 142.

[5] Köstenberger, *John*, 154.

[6] Scott, Jr., *Jewish Backgrounds to the New Testament*, 198. Given this background, it is not surprising the woman in John 4 asked Jesus about the proper place of worship. Christians often dismiss the question as a distractionary method because of ignorance of the history of the Samaritan Temple on Mount Gerizim. Interestingly, when Jesus was talking with the Samaritan woman, they would have easily been able to see Mount Gerizim.

[7] Ferguson, *Backgrounds of Early Christianity*, 428.

of Roman soldiers in Palestine was a reminder that the Jews were not independent. Additionally, Roman soldiers could enlist those they controlled to carry their equipment (Matt 5.41; 27.32), an oppressive practice which the Jews deeply resented but one with which they were forced to comply.[8]

A few passages from the New Testament might offer insight into Jew-Gentile relations in the First Century. In John 7.35, the Jews questioned Jesus' allusion to His pending departure: "Where does this man intend to go that we will not find Him? He is not intending to go to the Dispersion among the Greeks, and teach the Greeks, is He?" The implication seems to be Jesus could hide from them and their murderous intentions if He went into Gentile territory. They would never dream of following him into territory occupied by heathens.

In Acts 21, Paul returns from his third missionary journey and many false rumors have been spread about his teaching (Acts 21.20–21). Paul was with Trophimus the Ephesian in Jerusalem and the Jews (assuming Paul had brought a Gentile into the Temple) yells, "Men of Israel, come to our aid! This is the man who preaches to all men everywhere against our people and the Law and this place; and besides he has even brought Greeks into the temple and has defiled this holy place" (Acts 21.28). The crowd listens to Paul's defense because he speaks in Hebrew (Acts 21.40), but refuses to listen further when he informs them that God has commissioned him to preach to the Gentiles (Acts 22.21–22). Because of Paul's willingness to preach to Gentiles, they shout: "Away with such a fellow from the earth, for he should not be allowed to live" (Acts 22.22)!

From this information, one can deduce the Jew-Gentile relationship was strained. Gentiles might have had some hostile feelings toward Jews, but Jews clearly sought to limit their dealings with Gentiles. As is often the case, these cultural struggles spilled

---

[8] France, *The Gospel of Matthew*, NICNT, 222.

over into the early church. How would early Christianity deal with the animosity between Jews and Gentiles?

2.1.3 The Early Church Struggles with Gentile Relations

The early church had its fair share of questions about if, and on what terms, Gentiles should be accepted. In Acts 10, Peter went to speak with a Gentile centurion named Cornelius. Upon meeting him Peter said, "You yourselves know how unlawful it is for a man who is a Jew to associate with a foreigner or to visit him; and yet God has shown me that I should not call any man unholy or unclean. That is why I came without even raising any objection when I was sent for. So, I ask for what reason you have sent for me" (Acts 10.28–29). After hearing about Cornelius' vision, Peter preached Jesus to Cornelius and those who he had gathered to hear the good news (Acts 10.34–43).

When Peter returned to Jerusalem, several Jews took issue with him because he entered the home of a Gentile and ate with them (Acts 11.2–3). After Peter explained how God directed him, the objectors glorified God for providing salvation to the Gentiles (Acts 11.18).

The issue re-surfaced in a slightly different way in Acts 15 and Galatians 2.[9] The Jewish Christians attempted to bind the requirements of the Law of Moses upon the Gentile converts: "But some of the sect of the Pharisees who had believed stood up, saying, 'It is necessary to circumcise them and to direct them to observe the Law of Moses'" (Acts 15.5). The "Jerusalem Conference" in Acts 15 sought to settle the question and hear the testimony of Peter, Paul, and Barnabas. James, the brother of Jesus, spoke up, emphasizing his agreement with the Jewish prophets. They decided not to burden the Gentiles with observance of the law but gave them a few commands which would

---

[9] For our purposes, we will not comment on if these two accounts are the same event but simply highlight the problems this issue created for the early church.

allow table fellowship to be shared between Jew and Gentile converts to Christianity.[10]

Clearly, the inclusion of Gentiles was a contentious issue for the early church.[11] How should a largely Jewish community deal with outsiders? As followers of Jesus, one must inquire how Jesus dealt with Gentiles. Matthew's gospel does much to give a likely Jewish audience valuable examples and teaching, so they might effectively reach out to Gentiles and properly navigate Jew-Gentile relations.

2.3 Women in the First Century

The women of the First Century were largely homemakers.[12] Some wealthier homes might have contained separate quarters for men and women, but the average house of First Century Palestine would have seen much mingling of the genders.[13] Women's main duties were grinding flour, cooking, cleaning, making beds, doing laundry, spinning wool, bearing children, breastfeeding the children for the first two years, and childrearing.[14] A Jewish woman was even expected to wash her husband's face, hands, and feet.[15] Each sex was thought to have a God-assigned sphere and

---

[10] It seems that the purpose of the food law in the Jewish Scriptures was to keep the Jews distinct from all other nations (Lev 20.24–26). Thus, when Jesus declared all foods clean (Mark 7.18–19) it was a subtle way to show there was no distinction between Jew and Gentile.

[11] K.R. Iverson, "Gentiles" in *Dictionary of Jesus and the Gospels*, 2nd Edition. Editors Joel B. Green, Jeannine K. Brown, & Nicholas Perrin (Downers Grove: IVP Academic, 2013), 302–309.

[12] Stuart L. Love, *Jesus and Marginal Women: The Gospel of Matthew in Social-Scientific Perspective*, (Eugene: Cascade Books, 2009), 35.

[13] Spencer, "Women" in *Dictionary of Jesus and the Gospels*, 1005.

[14] Ben Witherington, *Women and the Genesis of Christianity* (New York: Cambridge University Press, 1990), 5. For further reading on this topic, read chapters 1–3 of Witherington's book in which he covers women's roles in Judaism, Hellenistic, and Roman settings.

[15] Witherington, *Women and the Genesis of Christianity*, 5.

was expected to behave appropriately in their sphere.[16] Hierocles[17] said, "They should be divided in the usual manner; namely, to the husband should be assigned those which have to do with agriculture, commerce, and the affairs of the city; to the wife those which have to do with spinning and the preparation of food, in short, those of a domestic nature" ("On Duties," *Household Management*, 4.28.21; 5.696, 15).

Xeneophon[18] added,

> Thus, to the woman, it is more honorable to stay indoors than to abide in the fields, but to the man it is unseemly rather to stay indoors than to attend to the work outside. If a man acts contrary to the nature God has given him, possibly his defiance is detected by the gods and he is punished for neglecting his own work or meddling with his wife's (*Concerning Household Management*, 7.3–10.13).

While the home might have been their sphere of duty, women were not confined there but often went out into the marketplace to shop and participate in life with the community.[19] A productive wife was an economic, social, and political asset,[20] but the public realm was male dominated.[21] Other than a few privileged women like Herodias (Matt 14.3), Drusilla (Acts 24.24), and Bernice (Acts 25.23; 26.30), women's role in politics seems to have been very restricted.[22] Pliny the younger wrote a letter in which he said his wife listened to his public presentations while

---

[16] Love, *Jesus and Marginal Women*, 36.

[17] Hierocles (AD 100–150) was a stoic but little is known about his life.

[18] Xeneophon (430–354 BC) was a Greek philosopher and historian.

[19] F. S. Spencer, "Women" in *Dictionary of Jesus and the Gospels*. 2nd Edition. Editors by Joel B. Green, Jeannine K. Brown, & Nicholas Perrin (Downers Grove: IVP Academic, 2013), 1004–1013.

[20] Love, *Jesus and Marginal Women*, 36.

[21] Ibid, 37.

[22] Spencer, "Women" in *Dictionary of Jesus and the Gospels*, 1005.

she was "concealed behind a curtain" (*Ep.* 4.19). Valerius Maximus asked and answered his own question about women in public life when he wrote, "What have women to do with a public assembly? If old-established custom is preserved, nothing" (*Fact. Et Dic.* 3.8.6). According to Plutarch,[23] women were to refrain from wine and "were not to speak, even on the most necessary of topics, unless their husbands were with them" (*Lycurgus and Numa* 3.5).[24] Even if her husband was present, public debate was considered "unbecoming behavior" for a woman.[25] While permitted to speak with her husband at her side, women were not allowed to engage in intellectual debates in society.

In the Apocryphal book of The Wisdom of Jesus, Son of Sirach, the author makes an interesting remark about the morality of women. The author identified himself as Jesus ben Eleazar ben Sira (Ben Sira 50.27) and is thought to have written in Jerusalem sometime between 195–170 BC.[26] Our author states, "Better is the wickedness of a man than a woman who does good; it is woman who brings shame and disgrace" (Ben Sira 42.14).[27] How representative this man's views were is impossible

---

[23] L. Mestrius Plutarchus (AD c. 45-c.120), better known as Plutarch, was a philosopher at the Academy founded by Plato and an avid writer. He wrote more than sixty biographies and about fifty of them have survived. For more information about his life, see Michael R. Licona, *Why are there Differences in the Gospels? What We can Learn from Ancient Biography* (Oxford: University Press, 2017), 15–16.

[24] Love, *Jesus and Marginal Women*, 38.

[25] Ibid, 38.

[26] Joanna K. Vitale, "A Comparative Analysis of Depictions of Female Beauty in the Hebrew Bible and the Jewish Apocrypha and Pseudepigrapha" (DPhil Thesis, Worcester College at the University of Oxford, 2015), 49.

[27] Ibid, 54. It should be noted this statement comes in a context of how a daughter is cause for constant anxiety for a father (Ben Sira 42.x). There are concerns over her sexual morality, being an embarrassment to the family, and parading her beauty before men.

to know, but it is safe to say that some Jews viewed women as morally suspect.

However, women were not complete outcasts in the First Century. Some women ran successful businesses, as illustrated by Lydia from Thyatira who sold purple fabrics (Acts 16.14) and Priscilla who worked with her husband, Aquila, as a tent maker (Acts 18.2–3). When the husband was away on a trip or business, the wife was expected to run the affairs of the house.[28] Roman men were often absent from the home, especially if they served in the military, which resulted in the wife being the actual head of the house and business manager.[29] However, among the elite, for the wife to earn an income would most likely have brought public dishonor upon her husband.[30]

Women's rights were very restricted in the First Century. Infant girls, much more than boys, were often exposed to the elements after birth to die.[31] Jewish women were not permitted to appear as a witness in a court of law[32] and were often ceremonially unclean. Few women learned to read and write, although there is some evidence for female scribes.[33] Advanced education was made available mainly to males through religious institutions.[34] The Talmud states, "Women, slaves, and minors are free from the obligation of Torah study" (*Talmud Torah* 1.1). A woman who studies the Torah is blessed but not as much as a man. A father is allowed but discouraged from teaching his daughter the Torah because she will not concentrate on her studies and, due to their lack of intelligence, turn the Torah into foolishness

---

[28] Ferguson, *Backgrounds of Early Christianity*, 77–78

[29] Witherington, *Women and the Genesis of Christianity*, 22.

[30] Love, *Jesus and Marginal Women*, 37.

[31] Witherington, *Women and the Genesis of Christianity*, 11 and 32.

[32] Ferguson, *Backgrounds of Early Christianity*, 78.

[33] Love, *Jesus and Marginal Women*, 39. He cites "beautiful handwriting" as evidence of some female scribes.

[34] Ibid, 39.

(*Talmud Torah* 1.13). Jewish rabbis of Jesus' day would have considered women as intellectually weak[35] and not allowed a woman to be among their disciples.[36] On the other hand, some Romans viewed female education favorably.[37]

John 4 contains one of the few New Testament statements about attitudes toward women. Jesus encounters the Samaritan woman at the well while the disciples enter the town to get Jesus something to eat. When they return, "they are amazed that He had been speaking with a woman, yet no one said, 'What do You seek?' or, 'Why do You speak with her?'" (John 4.27).[38] Thus, a Jew might question if women would be welcome into the fold of God's Kingdom.

These brief discussions of Gentiles and women in the First Century might show some of the questions a Christian Jewish community might have about accepting and reaching out to these groups. Matthew's gospel gives this community various examples of how Jesus dealt with each group as an example of what He expected the Church's mission to be: inviting everyone to receive the salvation He offers. Now our attention must be turned to cementing these two ideas into one cohesive theme.

---

[35] Tigay, *Deuteronomy*, 292.

[36] Craig S. Keener, *The Gospel of Matthew*, A Socio-Rhetorical Commentary (Grand Rapids: William B Eerdmans Publishing Company, 2009), 689. See also Darrell L. Bock, *Luke 9.51–24.53*, Baker Exegetical Commentary on the New Testament (Grand Rapids: Baker Academic, 1996), 1040.

[37] Witherington, *Women and the Genesis of Christianity*, 21.

[38] The woman in John 4 was surprised Jesus spoke to her because of her ethnicity (John 4.9), but the disciples do not mention that she was a Samaritan. They were surprised Jesus would speak to a woman (John 4.27).

III
THE MIXING OF THE GENTILE AND WOMEN'S THEME IN MATTHEW

To see a unified theme of inclusion in the gospel of Matthew, it would be helpful (if not necessary) to show how the inclusion of Gentiles and women are often intertwined in the text. The examples given here will be examined in closer detail shortly, but for now consider the following passages and see how the inclusion of Gentiles and women serves to show a larger theme of inclusion for all who would believe in the gospel of Jesus Christ.

3.1 Matthew 1.1–17
Matthew opens his book with a genealogy identifying Jesus as the descendant of Abraham, through whom God promised to bless the entire world (Gen 12.3). Just a few verses later there are four women who are highlighted: Tamar, Rahab, Ruth, and Bathsheba.[1] These women had strong non-Israelite roots. Tamar and Rahab were Canaanites, Ruth was a Moabite, and while Bathsheba's ethnicity is not known, she is identified as the "wife of Uriah" (1.6), who was a Hittite (2 Sam 23.39). The line of Christ

---

[1] For our current purposes there will be no discussion of Mary here. She plays an important role in the chapter and to the women who are presented, but since she was a Jew she does not assist us with connecting the Gentile and woman themes.

is traced through foreign women and illustrates how Abraham's seed would bless the world. From the opening chapter of the gospel, these two themes are presented as one.

3.2 Matthew 8.5–15

Matthew 8–9 witnesses Jesus as He graciously includes many outsiders. He heals a leper (8.1–4), cures two demon-possessed men who lived in the Gadarenes, calls a tax collector to follow him (9.9), eats with sinners (9.10–13), heals a woman with a flow of blood, raises a young girl from the dead (9.18–26), and opens the eyes of two blind men (9.27–31). The chapter closes with Jesus teaching and telling His disciples to pray for workers to be sent out to the lost sheep.

Within these chapters, the clearest example of inclusion is seen when Jesus heals the centurion's servant. The centurion realizes Jesus possesses authority and could heal from a distance. He requests Jesus simply say the word and the sickness would obey Him. Jesus marvels at his faith, stating he has not seen faith like this among anyone in Israel. Jesus sees the faith of this Gentile as looking forward to the Messianic banquet which would include Gentiles (8.11–12).

Immediately following the healing of the centurion's servant, the next account records the healing of Peter's mother-in-Law. In Matthew, Jesus takes the initiative in healing this woman. He is concerned about her and heals her. Perhaps Matthew is attempting to show that both Gentiles and women will be included in God's Kingdom by recording healings from these two groups back to back.

3.3 Matthew 12.38–42

The Pharisees challenge Jesus concerning His actions on the Sabbath day (12.1–14), but Jesus' miracles bring him attention and make the religious leaders intensely jealous. They claim His miracles are accomplished only by the power of Satan (12.24). Jesus shows the folly of this argument and condemns the religious leader's words (12.25–37).

After this stinging rebuke, the religious leaders request Jesus provide a sign to verify He is from God (12.38). Jesus calls them an "evil and adulterous generation" and would only give them the sign of Jonah the prophet (12.39–40).[2] Then Jesus identifies a group of Gentiles and a woman who would condemn this unbelieving generation.

In keeping with the "sign of Jonah," Jesus says the *men of Nineveh* would condemn this generation because they repented when Jonah preached. Jonah offered no signs and did not give the people any hope (see his message in Jonah 3.5), but they repented. Next, Jesus appeals to the "Queen of the South" (or Queen of Sheba) who came from the ends of the earth to listen to Solomon's wisdom. Both the *men of Nineveh* and the Queen of the South were Gentiles, but Matthew highlights the positive response of both male and female Gentiles to the message of God as an example for the Jews to follow.

3.4 Matthew 15.21–28

This episode has drawn much attention due to Jesus' original response to this woman. It will be covered in greater detail in chapters 4 and 5 since it combines both themes and raises the question of why Matthew would include negative statements about Gentiles in his gospel.

The section begins with the geographical note that Jesus entered the "district of Tyre and Sidon" (15.21). News of Jesus' miracles has spread through this region (4.24). A Canaanite woman approaches Him, requesting healing for her daughter who is suffering from demon possession. After some debate, Jesus heals her daughter and praises her for her faith.

---

[2] The sign of Jonah is clearly meant to point to Jesus' resurrection, which the religious leaders work together to cover up (28.11–15).

Mark describes the woman as "a Gentile, of the Syrophoenician race" (Mark 7.26). Matthew's description of her as the less technical "Canaanite" is probably meant to connect the woman with the pre-Israelite inhabitants of the land. The gospel is open to outsiders like this Canaanite woman.

3.5 Matthew 27.19

In the midst of the religious leaders stirring up the crowd to call for Jesus' crucifixion, there is one voice calling for him to be released: Pilate's wife. She had a dream about Jesus the previous night and realizes Jesus was a righteous man worthy of release. The lone dissenting voice of the crowds is an un-named Gentile woman.

3.6 Matthew 27.54–56

One final story should be highlighted. When Jesus died, Matthew recorded two unique events: an earthquake and the resurrection of some saints who appeared to many after Jesus' resurrection. After seeing the earthquake and the other events which surrounded His death the centurion said, "Truly this was the Son of God!" The "centurion's confession" at the end of the book replaces Peter's confession in Matthew 16.

The very next verse informs the reader that many women have followed Jesus from the start of His ministry and watched these events transpire from a distance. They seek to stand near Jesus in His darkest hour. They see where he is buried (27.61) and attempt to anoint his body after the Sabbath (28.1). The Gentile soldier's confession is described in the same breath as the women who stayed near to watch the horrific events of Jesus' suffering.

3.7 Conclusion

The theme of Gentiles and women being welcomed into the kingdom of God is more connected than one might think. From the examples we have examined, these themes have been intertwined in a variety of ways. Additionally, the above material is not focused in one small section but is peppered throughout the whole book from beginning to end. We now turn our attention to examining each of these themes in turn.

IV
GENTILE WOMEN AND INCLUSION IN MATTHEW

The story of Jesus, and the New Testament, begins with a genealogy requiring knowledge of the Jewish Scriptures. Modern day readers are usually disenchanted by a lengthy list of difficult names and may skip such sections of Scripture. But a book's beginning can provide insights into the authors' purpose by introducing central themes, major issues, or vital ideas to be expressed in the book.[1] A great example of this is Charles Dicken's timeless classic *A Christmas Carol* which opens with the dry statement, "Marley was dead to begin with. There is no doubt about that."[2] After repeating this fact multiple times, Dickens states clearly, "There is no doubt that Marley was dead. This must be distinctly understood, or nothing wonderful can come of the story that I am about to relate."[3] What insights can be gleaned from this genealogy about this Matthean theme?

---

[1] Nancy Declaisse-Walford, Rolf A. Jacobson, and Beth L. Tanner, *The Book of Psalms*, New International Commentary on the OT (Grand Rapids: William B. Eerdmans Publishing Company, 2014), 56. Iain Provan, *Seriously Dangerous Religion: What the Old Testament says and why it Matters* (Waco, TX: Baylor University Press, 2014), 59.

[2] Charles Dickens, *A Christmas Carol* (New Jersey: Watermill Press, 1980), 1.

[3] Dickens, *A Christmas Carol*, 2. Interestingly, Dickens goes on to establish his point by referencing the play *Hamlet*. He states that one must understand the beginning of the play and that Hamlet's father was dead or the story will have no meaning to the observer.

4.1 Matthew 1.1

Matthew and Luke both include genealogies in their telling of the story of Jesus. Matthew uses a descending genealogy, starting with Abraham and going down to Jesus, while Luke employs an ascending genealogy, starting with Jesus and going to Adam.[4] Matthew 1.1 reads, "The record of the genealogy of Jesus the Messiah the son of David, the son of Abraham." Matthew employs telescoping[5] to highlight two main Jewish characters Jesus descended from: Abraham and David. There are several reasons Matthew wanted to highlight these Jewish heroes,[6] but for our purposes our focus will rest on Abraham and David's connection with foreigners.

God calls Abram (his name was changed to Abraham in Genesis 17) when he is living in Ur of the Chaldeans (Gen. 11.31) and instructs him to go to the land God would show him (Gen. 12.1). God promises to turn Abram, a 75-year-old childless man (Gen. 12.4), into a mighty nation, to make his name great, and bless or curse people based on how they treat him. At the conclusion of God's promises to Abram God said, "And in you all the families of the earth will be blessed" (Gen 12.3b). God's plan is not simply to make Abram the father of the Jewish nation but to bless the whole world through him! Later in Genesis 22.18, God again promises to bless "all the nations of the earth" through Abraham's

---

[4]There are several differences between Matthew and Luke's genealogy. Luke wants to emphasis Jesus is the Son of God while Matthew seems to speak to the inclusion of Gentiles. This reminds the reader biblical authors often record the same things but with a different theological point in mind.

[5]Telescoping is a literary device used in genealogies to skip over a large section of people but connect an individual with a famous or heroic ancestor.

[6]Abraham was the father of the nation and many of the Jews expected the Messiah to come from the line of David (22.41–42). Jesus will often be called the "Son of David" in the gospel (1.1; 9.27; 12.23; 15.22; 20.30–31; 21.9, 15; 22.42) all with messianic overtones.

seed.[7] As the Messiah and the descendant of Abraham (1.1), Jesus will be the means through which this promise is fulfilled.

In Genesis 17, God establishes the covenant of circumcision with Abraham and his descendants forever. For all coming generations, this is the mark of the covenant between God and Abraham: every male eight days and older would be circumcised (Gen 17.10–12). Failure to be circumcised would result in being cut off from the people. God's covenant is not limited to the line of Israel but was open to the "foreigner" or servant who was born or purchased (Gen 17.12–13, 27). From God's founding of the Jewish nation, outsiders are welcomed to come into a covenant relationship with God. Jesus coming from the line of Abraham reminds the reader his new covenant will be open to all people. By alluding to Abraham, Matthew wants his readers to remember God's promises to him and prepare them for Jesus' final instruction in the gospel: the great commission (28.18–20).[8]

More than Abraham, Matthew seeks to draw a link between Jesus and David. David appears in 1.1 and is the only one in the genealogy given the title of King (1.6). Lastly, the genealogy seems to be divided around David and Jesus (1.17).[9] Throughout the gospel, Jesus is referred to as the "son of David" seven times (9.27; 12.23; 15.22; 20.30–31; 21.9, 15)[10] compared to twice in Mark (Mark 10.47–48) and Luke (Luke 18.38–39), while John never employs the phrase.

---

[7] Paul picks up on the singular "seed" in Galatians 3.16 and states it was a prophecy that Jesus would be a blessing to all nations.

[8] John C. Hutchison, "Women, Gentiles, and the Messianic Mission in Matthew's Genealogy" *Bibliotheca Sacra* 158 no. 630 (2001), 152–164.

[9] Even the number 14 could be a reference to David since the numeric value of David's name in Hebrew is 14. Matthew clearly omits some generations to get to the number 14 in each division.

[10] It is used 9 times total. Once of Joseph (1.20) and once when Jesus asked the crowds whose son the Messiah would be (22.42).

While Abraham's connections to the Gentile mission were obvious, David also has a few. All genealogies show David's great-grandmother was Ruth (Ruth 4.17–22; 1 Chron 2.11–12; Matt 1.5) who was a Moabite (Ruth 1.4). The family connection is strong enough that David leaves his parents in the protective custody of the King of Moab when he is fleeing from Saul (1 Sam 22.3–4). Later when David's mighty men are listed, they contain two Gentiles: Zelek the Ammonite (1 Sam. 23.37) and Uriah the Hittite (1 Sam 23.39).

Additionally, the use of "son of David" is found in some contexts which seem to look forward to a Gentile mission. In 12.23, the crowd wonders if Jesus could be the "son of David." This occurs right after Matthew states Jesus fulfills Isaiah 42, which included taking His message to the Gentiles (12.18, 21). A Canaanite woman begging Jesus to heal her daughter addresses Jesus as "son of David" (15.22) and her request is granted. When Jesus enters Jerusalem, the crowds chant "son of David" (21.9), a fact which offends the religious leaders (21.15). In between these two references, Jesus cleanses the temple, quotes from Isaiah 56.7 and Jeremiah 7.11, and reminds people the temple is to be a house of prayer. When Isaiah 56.7 is read in full it informs the reader that God's temple is to be a house of prayer for *all nations*.

The telescoping employed by Matthew to highlight both Abraham and David is not merely to show Jesus' Jewish roots, but to connect Jesus as the fulfillment of the promises to these two men. Jesus would bless the world with his death and resurrection and replace the temple (built by a descendant of David) as the ultimate place of worship for all people.

4.2 Matthew 1.2–17

Generally, in Jewish genealogies the line is traced from father to son (Gen 5, 36; 1 Chron 1–9; Luke 3.23–38) and women rarely make an appearance.[11] This is evident when Matthew and Luke's

---

[11] Hutchison, "Women, Gentiles, and the Messianic Mission in Mat-

genealogy are compared and Luke included no women, not even Mary.[12] Sometimes, as when Judah returned from Babylonian captivity, the purpose of Jewish genealogies was to establish racial purity (Ezra 2.59–63; Neh 7.63–65). The fact that Matthew includes five women, most of whom were Gentiles, in the line of Jesus would have been shocking to his Jewish audience.[13] Why do these five women—Tamar, Rahab, Ruth, Bathsheba, and Mary—obtain a prominent position in the line of Christ?

Perhaps the most popular view is that these women all have a questionably sexual past. Tamar, a Canaanite, poses as a prostitute and seduces her father-in-law Judah after she realizes Judah is not going to keep his word and give his third son Shelah to her as a husband (Gen 38.12–19). Due to this encounter she is impregnated and has twins (Gen 38.18, 24–29). Rahab is continually described as a harlot, her occupation in Jericho (Josh 2.1; 6.25; Heb 11.31; James 2.25), even though she ceased this practice once she joined the nation of Israel. Ruth's actions at the threshing floor would have raised eyebrows based on Boaz sending her away early in the morning before she could be seen (Ruth 3.6–9). Bathsheba committed adultery with David in one of the most well-known sins in all of Biblical history (2 Sam 11). Lastly, Mary is not even off the hook as many who knew her would have drawn the same conclusions that Joseph did before the angel appeared to him (Matt 1.19).

While this is a compelling narrative to some, and certainly does have some thoughtful points, I would like to suggest these women are highlighted because they point toward Gentile in-

thew's Genealogy" *Bibliotheca Sacra*, 163. He does give a few exceptions to this in the Jewish scriptures (Gen 11.29; 22.20–24; 25.1; 35.22–26; 36.10, 22; 1 Cor 2.4, 18–21, 24, 34, 46–49; 7.24).

[12] Wong, "The Gentiles and Gentile Mission in the Gospel of Matthew," M.A. Thesis, 32.

[13] J. Daniel Hays, *From Every People and Nation: A Biblical Theology of Race* (Downers Grover: InterVarsity Press, 2003), 159.

clusion or speak of a Gentile showing great faith.[14] Especially interestingly, is some of these Gentile women displayed extraordinary faith while the Jews in the story lacked faith. This would fit Matthew's overall theme better than highlighting the sexual mistakes of past, foreign women. Matthew's gospel depicts two people as having great faith, both are Gentiles and one is a woman (8.10; 15.28). Matthew concludes by depicting Jesus' women followers as showing great faith and loyalty to him. We now will examine each of these women to see if Gentile inclusion or Gentile faith can be found.

Tamar (1.3) is a Canaanite whose story appears in Genesis 38. In some ways this story shows us God's grace since no character emerges from the story looking very holy. Er (Gen 38.7) and Onan (Gen 38.9–10) are struck by the Lord because of their wickedness. Judah lies to Tamar; he has no intention to give his third son, Shelah, to Tamar since his other two sons have died while married to her (Gen 38.11, 14). Judah then sleeps with who he believes is a prostitute but is actually Tamar in disguise (Gen 38.14–19). Both Judah and Tamar deceive each other and engage in immoral activity together.

Despite the rampant sinful behavior described in Genesis 38, Judah states that Tamar was more righteous than him (Gen 38.26). Seeing the failures committed by Judah in Genesis 37–38, this may not serve as the most powerful of endorsements; but by the time of Ruth, Tamar does seem to be pictured more positively. In Ruth 4.12, the people of Bethlehem bless Ruth and Boaz's union by saying, "Moreover, may your house be like the house of Perez whom Tamar bore to Judah, through the offspring which the LORD will give you by this young woman."

While neither of these passages might cause us to pronounce Tamar a woman of faith, ancient Christian interpretation of

---

[14]Hutchison, "Women, Gentiles, and the Messianic Mission in Matthew's Genealogy" *Bibliotheca Sacra*, 153.

Tamar's birth story was said to point forward to Gentiles being welcomed into God's kingdom. According to an ancient, anonymous homily on Matthew 1, Tamar's twins, Zerah and Perez, are symbolic of how the Jews were first God's people and Gentile inclusion occurred later. Zerah symbolized the Jewish nation since his arm emerged from the birth canal first and was marked with the scarlet thread of circumcision. Perez being born first symbolized how the Gentiles came to faith first in the New Covenant. Zerah's birth symbolized how Paul explained the Jews would eventually accept Jesus as the Messiah (Rom 11.25–26).[15]

The next woman in Matthew's genealogy is Rahab (1.5). Her story is contained in Joshua 2.1–21 and 6.17, 22–25. While Rahab had the same information that every other inhabitant of Jericho did, she uniquely responded in faith (Josh 2.8–11). Rahab expressed faith that God would give Israel not only Jericho but all the land of Canaan. Her faith stands in stark contrast to the wilderness generation who refused to take the land, thinking they could not overcome the giants and the strongly fortified cities which existed in Canaan (Num 13–14). She is twice remembered in the New Testament as a hero of faith (Heb 11.31; James 2.25), listed in the same breath as several Jewish heroes. Interestingly, Matthew is the only Biblical author not to mention she once was a harlot (compare Matt 1.5 with Josh 2.1; 6.22, 25; Heb 11.31; James 2.25).[16]

Rahab is not only a woman of faith who spared her family from destruction, she is a picture of inclusion into the Jewish nation. As the narrative of Joshua 6 comes to a conclusion the author notes, "However, Rahab the harlot and her father's house-

---

[15] Manlio Simonetti (Ed.), *Ancient Christian Commentary on Scripture: Matthew 1–13*, New Testament 1a (Downers Grove: InterVarsity Press, 2001), 6–7.

[16] In Joshua 6.22, she is simply called the harlot with no reference to her name. Here Matthew simply calls her by name with no reference to her former profession.

hold and all she had, Joshua spared; and she has lived in the midst of Israel to this day, for she hid the messengers whom Joshua sent to spy out Jericho" (Josh 6.25). Rahab is spared from the destruction of Jericho, and is received by the people of God.

Third, Ruth is mentioned (1.5). Her story is told in the book which bears her name. Elimelech, Naomi, Mahlon, and Chilion leave Bethlehem because of a famine and live in the land of Moab (Ruth 1.1–2). During their stay, Elimelech dies (Ruth 1.3) and the boys marry Moabite women (Ruth 1.4). Ruth marries Mahlon (Ruth 4.10) and Chilion marries Orpah. Sadly, Mahlon and Chilion both die (Ruth 1.5) and Naomi decides to return to Bethlehem. At first, both Orpah and Ruth intend to return with her, but Naomi convinces Orpah to stay. Despite her best effort to convince Ruth to stay in Moab with Orpah, Ruth refuses to leave her mother-in-law. Ruth's faith and loyalty are truly admirable. She leaves behind everything she knows to serve her mother-in-law (Ruth 2.11) and is recognized by all as a woman of excellence (Ruth 3.11).[17] The story takes place during the time of the Judges (Ruth 1.1), which was a time Israel often fell into the sin of idolatry. While Israel often forsook the worship of Yahweh for idols, Ruth surrendered her polytheistic ways for the worship of Yahweh (Ruth 1.15–16).

Bathsheba, who "had been the wife of Uriah" appears fourth (1.6). Uriah is often described as "Uriah the Hittite,"[18] and it is possible Bathsheba shared the same ethnicity as her husband, making her a foreigner as well.[19] However, it is equally possible she was a Jew. Her grandfather is Ahithophel (2 Sam 11.3;

---

[17] This is the same word (Hebrew *chayil*) used to describe the excellent woman in 31.10, 29. Ruth is truly an example of the virtuous woman.

[18] 2 Sam 11.3,6, 17, 21, 24; 12.9–10; 23.29; 1 Kgs 15.5; 1 Chron. 11.41.

[19] According to the author of Chronicles both Judah's wife, who was a Canaanite, and Bathsheba had the same name (1 Chron 2.3; 3.5). This may give further evidence that Bathsheba was indeed a Gentile.

23.34) who seems to be an Israelite from the tribe of Judah (Josh 15.51; 2 Sam 15.12).

Perhaps Matthew brings up Bathsheba to spotlight Uriah. Bathsheba is described as the former "wife of Uriah" probably to highlight Uriah's faith in contrast to King David's failure of faith.[20] After all, Uriah is unimportant in the genealogy since no one is traced through him, but there are two ways in which his inclusion and his faithfulness are seen. First, he is a clear picture of Gentile inclusion among God's people. Despite being repeatedly referred to as a Hittite he is one of David's mighty men (2 Sam 23.39; 1 Chron 11.41). Second, we see Uriah's faithfulness in his concern for God and others. David tries to cover up his sin by bringing home Uriah from battle, hoping he would sleep with Bathsheba and think the child was his (2 Sam 11.1–8). Uriah refuses to enjoy the pleasures of home when the ark of the Lord was in temporary shelters and the king's army was engaged in a fierce battle (2 Sam 11.11). Once it was David who was concerned about enjoying the pleasures of a beautiful home while the ark of God was only inside a tent (2 Sam 7.2), but now it is Uriah the Hittite who is concerned for the ark of the Lord. David makes Uriah drunk, hoping that will entice him to go to his house, but Uriah has more moral qualms drunk than David does sober and once more refuses to go to home (2 Sam 12.13). David sees no other alternative than to send this faithful servant to his death and entrusts Uriah with carrying his own execution note (2 Sam 11.14–15). Uriah the Hittite is concerned with the ark of the Lord, the people of the Lord, and being faithful to David while King David violates several of God's ten commandments to cover his sin.

Lastly, Mary the mother of Jesus is mentioned (1.16). While Mary was Jewish, the theme of God working through women

---

[20] Hutchison, "Women, Gentiles, and the Messianic Mission in Matthew's Genealogy" *Bibliotheca Sacra*, 153, 160.

to accomplish his message of salvation is still present. Recall from chapter 3 how Matthew intertwines Gentile and women inclusion, and this seems to be evident here. It is Luke's gospel that highlights Mary's faith and attitude, but Matthew speaks of Mary giving birth to the Messiah (1.17) and being married to Joseph (1.17). While none of Mary's story is told by Matthew, we see her husband is a righteous man (1.19) who faithfully obeys the Lord (1.24; 2.13–15). While Mary's faith is not specifically highlighted, she is an important part to God's plan since she is the mother of the Messiah and marries a man who exudes faith.

Clearly, Matthew's genealogy is giving us insight into a major theme. The work of Jesus and the salvation he brings is for Jews and Gentiles regardless of gender. Jesus is a universal Savior who came to save his people (1.21) and all people (28.18–20) from their sins![21] In the story of the Jewish nation, Gentiles and women have been used by God all along to bring the gift of salvation to all people.[22] Jesus' genealogy highlights stories of Gentile and female faith,[23] a theme the reader will see throughout Matthew as Jesus praises Gentiles and women for their faith (8.10; 9.22; 15.28). Leon Morris gives a thought-provoking quote on genealogies. Morris states:

> [The Christian] will reflect that God's hand is over all history. God works out his purpose, generation after generation. Limited as we are to one lifetime, each of us sees so little of what happens. A genealogy is a striking way of bringing before us the continuity of God's purpose through the ages. The process of history is not haphazard. There is a purpose in it all. And the purpose is the purpose of God.[24]

---

[21] Samuel B. Hakh, "Women in the Genealogy of Matthew" *Exchange* 43 (2014), 109–118.

[22] Wim J. C. Weren, "The Five Women in Matthew's Genealogy" *Catholic Biblical Quarterly* 59 no. 2 (1997), 288–305.

[23] Hutchison, "Women, Gentiles, and the Messianic Mission in Matthew's Genealogy" *Bibliotheca Sacra*, 164.

[24] Arthur E. Cundall and Leon Morris, *Judges & Ruth: An Introduc-*

4.3 Matthew 2.1–12

In an account unique to Matthew, the first characters the read-er encounters after the birth of Jesus are Gentiles.[25] These Gen-tiles are Magi from the east, perhaps Babylon (1.17),[26] seeking to worship Jesus (2.2, 11).[27] They are the first human characters to speak and set the tone for the subsequent Gentiles characters[28]: "Where is He who has been born King of the Jews? For we saw His star in the east and have come to worship Him" (2.2). Israel had long awaited the coming of the Messiah, but it was Gentiles who announced His coming to the Jews![29] The gospel opens with Gentiles traversing a great distance to worship Jesus and closes with Jesus' commanding His disciples to travel a great distance to make disciples of all nations (28.18–20).

Additionally, the Magi's response to Jesus was meant to be contrasted with Herod the Great (37–4 BC) and Jerusalem's re-sponse to this new King. The Magi went on a long journey to worship Jesus and were overjoyed upon finding him (2.10), but Herod and Jerusalem were troubled by the announcement of this new King (2.3). The religious leaders, despite their abun-

---

tion and Commentary, Tyndale Old Testament Commentaries (Downers Grove: InterVarsity Press, 1968), 318.

[25] Gene Smillie, "'Even the Dogs': Gentiles in the Gospel of Mat-thew" *Journal of Evangelical Theological Society* 45 no. 1 (2002), 73–97.

[26] The Magi are generally thought to come either from Babylon or Persia. See France, *The Gospel of Matthew,* NICNT, 66–67; Michael J. Wilkins, *Matthew,* The NIV Application Commentary (Grand Rapids: Zondervan, 2004), 93. Smillie, "'Even the Dogs': Gentiles in the Gospel of Matthew" *JETS* 45 no. 1 (2002), 73–97 argues for Babylonian Magi since Babylon exile was emphasized in the genealogy.

[27] In the Jewish scriptures, "East" is often a direction that symbolizes moving away from God (Gen 2.24; 4.16; 13.11; Jonah 4.5) but here these individuals from the "East" come to worship God!

[28] Smillie, "'Even the Dogs': Gentiles in the Gospel of Matthew" *JETS,* 84.

[29] Wilkins, *Matthew,* NIV Application Commentary, 94.

dant knowledge of Scripture, were apathetic to the announcement of the Messiah while the Magi, with their limited knowledge, come with gifts[30] to worship the King of the World (2.2, 8).[31] These Magi were alert and watching for the Messiah; the Jews were not.

Joseph was a righteous man whom God directed with dreams (1.20–24; 2.13, 19, 22). Just as God guided Joseph through a dream to protect Jesus, so, too, He directed the Magi through a dream for the same purpose (2.12). In Matthew, Jews, Gentiles, and women (27.19) receive dreams from God, perhaps to indicate God welcoming all into His kingdom.

The material recorded in Matthew 1–2 is unique to his gospel.[32] He begins the story of Jesus by tracing His lineage through foreigners and women. Gentiles make the long journey to worship and present gifts to the newborn King. Matthew sees women and Gentiles as playing a significant role in Jesus' genealogy and early life. The author will continue to show these two groups playing a role in Jesus' ministry.

4.4 Matthew 4.1–11

Jesus' temptations and ability to overcome them by quoting from Deuteronomy illustrate Jesus succeeded where Israel failed. However, in the third temptation, the devil reveals a universal dimension to these temptations. Satan offers Jesus all the kingdoms of the world if Jesus would worship him. What a cruel offer. Jesus has laid aside His heavenly kingdom with the intention of gath-

---

[30] The gifts the Magi bestow upon the child are fitting for a King, but also hold great significance in the Jewish scriptures (1 Kgs 10.1–10; Pss 2, 72.8–15; Isa 60.1–9).

[31] David L. Turner, *Matthew*, Baker Exegetical Commentary on the New Testament (Grand Rapids: Baker Academic, 2008), 87.

[32] While Luke covers the Birth narrative of Jesus in greater detail his focus is on Mary while Matthew relates the story from Joseph's perspective.

ering all these nations into the Kingdom of God.[33] Satan, God's enemy, recognizes the universal implications of Jesus' ministry.

4.5 Matthew 4.12–25

John the Baptist's arrest (4.12) signals the beginning of Jesus' ministry (4.17). Upon hearing about John's arrest, Jesus withdraws into Galilee.[34] Jesus has been living in Nazareth since His youth (2.22–23) but moves to Capernaum which occupies the regions allotted to Zebulun and Naphtali in the Old Testament. Jesus' actions are depicted by Matthew as a fulfillment of Isaiah 9.1–2. Jesus' geographical movements fulfill Scripture.[35]

Matthew adds a significant detail to the Isaiah quotation by stating Jesus settled in "Galilee of the Gentiles" (4.15). Galilee has been in darkness too long and the Light of the World has come to shine in "Galilee of the Gentiles." It is here Jesus proclaims His message, "Repent, for the kingdom of heaven is at hand" (4.17).

In Galilee of the Gentiles, while walking by the sea (4.13, 18), Jesus calls his first disciples. Peter, Andrew, James, and John immediately accept Jesus' invitation to become fishers of men (4.19). The call to be fishers of men looks forward to the great commission (28.18–20). As Matthew concludes his gospel, Jesus appears on a mountain in Galilee (28.16) and commissions his followers to be fishers of men to the entire world.[36]

---

[33] Wilkins, *Matthew*, NIV Application Commentary, 160.

[34] Since Jesus ties His fate to John the Baptist's (17.9–13) every time something bad happens to John, Jesus withdraws (4.12; 14.12–13).

[35] Isaiah prophesied during 740–686 BC according to Isaiah 1.1. In 722 BC, Assyria took the Northern nation of Israel captive. Because of the geographical location of Israel armies always attacked from the North (with the exception of Egypt in 2 Chron. 12) which meant Zebulun and Naphtali would have borne the brunt of the invasion. Isaiah comforted the people who had been taken captive by telling them the savior was coming.

[36] Paul Hertig, "The Inclusive and Contextualized Mission of Jesus in the Gospel of Matthew" *Evangelical Theological Society Papers* (1999): 1–15.

Interestingly, although not mentioned until the end of the gospel, Galilee is where Jesus gains many female followers. As the women witness the events of Jesus' death, Matthew informs the reader many women "had followed Jesus from Galilee while ministering to Him" (27.55). Matthew sees Jesus beginning His ministry in Galilee as welcoming Gentiles and women.

Jesus' newfound popularity is due to His teaching and ability to heal every sickness brought to him (4.23). Regions outside of Galilee hear of His power over sickness and come seeking His healing hand. Large crowds follow him from Syria, Galilee, the Decapolis, Jerusalem, Judea, and beyond the Jordan. According to Josephus, Syria had a large Jewish population in Jesus' day (Josephus *War* 2.461–468), but the Decapolis region had a predominantly Gentile population and probably hints of Jesus' intention of an extensive Gentile mission.[37] Jesus' message is welcoming and attractive even to non-Jewish audiences.

4.6 Matthew 5–7

The Sermon on the Mount is generally noted for its negative statements about Gentiles, but, here, a few positive thoughts about Gentile inclusion from the sermon will be examined.[38]

4.6.1 Matthew 5.1

On account of the large crowd following Jesus (4.25), he ascends a mountain and directs his teaching to the disciples (5.1–2) although the crowd is still listening (4.25; 5.1; 7.28–29). It seems logical that the crowd which pursued Jesus in 4.23–25 would be the same crowd since the original Greek in 4.25 and 5.1 indicate no break in the story.[39]

---

[37] Keener, *The Gospel of Matthew*, 158–159.

[38] The negative statements about the Gentiles will be discussed section 5.2: *Negative uses of "Gentile" in Matthew 5.47; 6.7, 32; 18.17; 20.25.*

[39] Smillie, "'Even the Dogs': Gentiles in the Gospel of Matthew" *JETS*, 88.

Due to the demographics of the crowd, Jesus slightly alters His wording, so all present might be able to understand His teaching. When speaking with Jewish leaders or crowds Jesus would say, "It is written" (11.10; 21.13; 26.24, 31), "Have you not read" (12.3, 5; 19.4; 22.31), or "Isaiah [or one of the prophets] said" (13.14; 15.7; 22.43, 45; 24.15), but in the Sermon on the Mount He used the phrase, "You have heard" (5.21, 27, 33, 38, 43).[40] This phrase *only* appears in the Sermon on the Mount. Perhaps Jesus' use of the "you have heard it said" formula was designed to be inclusive and welcoming to those outside of Judaism.[41]

4.6.2 Matthew 5.13–16

Pliny said there is nothing more useful than salt and sunshine (*Natural History* 31.102) and these are the elements Jesus calls his disciple to be. However, Jesus' instruction to be salt and light is more than a call to be useful, but is a summons to a universal mission: Christians are the "salt of the *earth*" (5.13) and the "light of the *world*" (5.16). Christians must halt the decay of the world by preserving those they encounter just as salt does.[42] Interestingly, Jesus has just been described as fulfilling Isaiah 9.1–2 by bringing

---

[40] Smillie, "'Even the Dogs': Gentiles in the Gospel of Matthew" *JETS*, 89. See France, *The Gospel of Matthew*, NICNT 195 who points out this phrase does expect a quotation from the Jewish scriptures. First, the phrase "it was said" uses a rare form of a verb which is "used in the New Testament specifically for quotations of Scripture of divine pronouncements." Second, the traditions Jesus referred to had to be old since "the ancients" knew of them. Third, each of the quotes "is based on an identifiable passage or theme of the Pentateuch" except for 5.43, which adds the additional clause. Thus, France thinks the hearer/reader would "expect to find a quotation of the mosaic law" following the phrase, "You have heard." If Gentiles were present they probably would have expected a Jewish man to quote from the Jewish scriptures. However, why does Jesus depart from the traditional "It is written" only here? It seems plausible His use of this phrase was meant to be inclusive to a Gentile audience.

[41] Ibid, 89.

[42] Ibid, 59.

his light to "Galilee of the Gentiles." Jesus has come as the light to bring the entire world out of the darkness in which they were encased. He expects his followers to have that same world-wide mission in mind.

4.6.3 Matthew 7.28–29

While the sermon is addressed to His disciples, Jesus clearly wants all present to understand and accept His teaching (7.24–27). The crowds, including Gentiles, are potential disciples.[43] Jesus is willing to teach and heal anyone, but the response is up to them. The crowds are impressed with his teaching, but as was made clear from the Sermon on the Mount, Jesus demands more of an individual than amazement at his words.

4.7 Matthew 8.5–13

In the parallel account in Luke 7.1–10, the Jewish leaders approach Jesus to inform him of the centurion's kindness to the Jewish nation and for building the local synagogue (Luke 7.3–5). However, Matthew excludes all Jewish elements. The centurion comes on his own and pleads with Jesus for assistance. While we have argued for hints of Gentiles being present in Matthew 1–7, this is the first account in Matthew where the adult Jesus interacts with a Gentile.

This event takes place in Capernaum (8.5), which is where Jesus settled and began his earthly ministry (4.13). He heals every kind of disease brought to him (4.23) and, specifically, has healed paralytics (4.24). The centurion's servant is paralyzed and tormented (8.6) and he turns to Jesus knowing Jesus could heal his servant.[44]

Some scholars argue Jesus' response has been mistranslated and should be a question rather than a statement: "Am I to come and

---

[43] Keener, *The Gospel of Matthew*, 165.

[44] Suriya Wongratanamajcha, "The Gentiles in Matthew: An Exegesis on the Relationship of the Gentiles and Jesus" (Master Thesis, Lincoln Christian Seminary, 1998), 13.

heal him?"[45] Since Jews did not enter the homes of Gentiles (Acts 10.28; 11.3; see also John 18.28), Jesus would have objected to going to the home of the centurion. However, at the very least, the context shows that Jesus did not hesitate to heal those considered to be "outcasts."[46] In 8.1–15 we see three of Jesus' miracles. Jesus heals an excluded leper (8.1–4), a Gentile's servant (8.5–13), and a woman (8.14–15).[47] Additionally, Jesus has shown He departs from the normal Jewish standard by touching the leper and Peter's Mother-in-law. The Law of Moses declared the leper unclean and he was to announce that he was unclean to any who came near him (Lev. 13.45–46). Additionally, the Jewish Halakeah prohibited touching a person afflicted with a fever.[48] Rather than making Jesus unclean, his touch provides healing and cleansing for them!

The centurion responds by declaring himself unworthy and, due to Jesus' authority, insists the trip is unnecessary. All Jesus has to do is say the word and the disease would obey him (9.8–9). Jesus marveled that this Gentile possessed greater faith than he witnessed among the Jews. Jesus praises the centurion's faith, "whose flesh was alien but whose spirit was of the household of faith."[49]

Jesus' purpose is not simply to give this Gentile a compliment. This man shows insight to Jesus' identity which many in Israel lack. It prepares the reader for the declaration of another Gentile centurion who heeds the signs that others ignored.[50] Jesus'

---

[45] France, *The Gospel of Matthew*, NICNT, 312–314; Keener, *The Gospel of Matthew*, 266–267.

[46] Wongratanamajcha, "The Gentiles in Matthew" M. A. Thesis, 16.

[47] Kukzin Lee, "Jesus and the Gentiles in Matthew" (Master Thesis, Gordon-Conwell Theological Seminary, 1999), 37.

[48] D. A. Carson, "Matthew" in *The Expositor's Bible Commentary*, General Editor Frank E. Gaebelein (Grand Rapids: Zondervan Publishing House, 1984), 204.

[49] Quote from Augustine which appeared in Simonetti (Ed.), *Ancient Christian Commentary on Scripture: Matthew 1–13*, 163.

[50] Carson, "Matthew" in *EBC*, 202.

remarks concerning the greatness of the centurion's faith were addressed to those following him (8.10). In addition to praising this Gentile's faith, Jesus informs the crowds many "from east and west" would enjoy the Messianic banquet while the sons of the kingdom would be cast out into the darkness (8.11–12). The sons of the kingdom being cast out clearly refers to the Jews,[51] but who will travel from the east and west to enjoy the company of the Jewish patriarchs? In the context of Matthew, the answer is certainly the Gentiles. The reader will remember Matthew told of the Magi journeying from the east to worship Jesus (2.1–2). Next, the reader witnessed Jesus' forerunner presenting a similar message. When John the Baptist appears on the scene, he informs his listeners salvation does not occur because one is a physical descendent of Abraham (3.9).[52] Lastly, The Jewish Scriptures, which Matthew plays off of heavily, had foretold of the inclusion of the entire earth at the Messianic banquet (Isa 25.6–9; 56.3–8).[53] Jesus clearly implies Gentiles would engage in intimate, eternal table fellowship with the founders of the Jewish nation. Jesus announces Jews and Gentiles will enjoy God's presence for eternity. What an amazing, powerful picture of inclusion!

4.8 Matthew 8.14–15

The parallel accounts for this miracle can be found in Mark 1.29–31 and Luke 4.38–39. Peter's wife is never mentioned in the gospels, but his mother-in-law makes this brief appearance.[54]

---

[51] For more info see Wongratanamajcha, "The Gentiles in Matthew," 20–23; Turner, *Matthew*, BECNT, 233; Carson, "Matthew" in *EBC*, 202; Wilkins, *Matthew*, NIV Application Commentary, 343; and Keener, *The Gospel of Matthew*, 269.

[52] Robert H. Gundry, "Book of Matthew" in *Dictionary for Theological Interpretation of the Bible*. Editor Kevin J. Vanhoozer (Grand Rapids: Baker Academic, 2005), 486–491.

[53] Wilkins, *Matthew*, NIV Application Commentary, 342.

[54] Peter's wife is mentioned in 1 Corinthians 9.5, but she is not named and there is nothing substantial said about her other than the

She is suffering from some unnamed sickness which has caused her to be bedridden with a fever. While this account appears in the three synoptic gospels, Matthew gives one detail lacking in the other two gospels.

In Mark and Luke, Jesus heals Peter's mother-in-law only after others request it of him (Mark 1.30; Luke 4.38). In Matthew's account, Jesus notices the woman and takes the initiative to heal her. Since this account occurs immediately after Jesus healed the centurion's servant, where he discusses inclusion into the kingdom of heaven, perhaps it is a hint that just as the Gentiles are included in the Kingdom, women are as well.

4.9 Matthew 9.18–26

A synagogue official approaches Jesus, begging him to come raise his daughter from the dead. As they make their way to the little girl's home, a woman who has suffered from a hemorrhage for twelve years seeks healing from Jesus. According to the Law of Moses, this woman and everything she touched were unclean (Lev 15.25–26). Her hope was to simply touch Jesus' garment, be healed, and disappear back in the crowd. Despite the large crowd thronging around him, Jesus can distinguish someone's touch of faith, rather than a touch of curiosity or hostility.[55] Instead of rebuking the woman for being in a crowd with her unclean condition, Jesus affirms her as a "daughter" in God's house and praises her for her remarkable faith.[56] In Matthew, it is after Jesus praises her faith that she is healed from her twelve year

---

fact she accompanied Peter when he went out to preach. According to Eusebius 3.30.2, Peter witnessed his wife's execution and encouraged her during the process by "addressing her by name" and calling on her to remember the Lord. However, Eusebius does not state what her name was. Eusebius also informs us that Peter and his wife had children (3.30.1).

[55] Kenneth L. Chumbley, *The Gospel of Matthew* (Nashville: Self-Published, 1999), 179.

[56] F. S. Spencer. "Women" in *DJG*, 1007.

affliction. In the gospel thus far, a Gentile and a woman have been commended by Jesus for their faith.

The scene shifts back to the little girl and death permeates the air. The flute-players, mourners, and family create a chaotic scene. According to Jewish tradition, even the poorest of families had to hire two flute players and one wailing woman (Ketuboth 4.4; Josephus, *War* 3.9.5). Jesus dismisses the unruly crowd from their services, and mourning will not be needed since he has appeared. The little girl's death is real, but not final.[57] Jesus arouses her from death as easily as one would arouse someone from slumber. Most rabbis viewed the loss of a daughter as less significant than the loss of a son, but Jesus displays equal concern over the loss of either son or daughter (see Luke 7.11–17).[58]

In addition to highlighting the faith of a woman, this text might look forward to Jesus' own resurrection.[59] This is the first, and only, account in Matthew where Jesus specifically raises someone from the dead. He tells the messengers of John the Baptist to report all they have witnessed, which includes the raising of the dead (11.5). Jesus grants this power to the disciples (10.8), but there is no record of them performing such an act in this gospel. Given the uniqueness of the account in Matthew, it is probably significant.[60] Perhaps since Matthew presents Jesus restoring life first to a young woman, it anticipates how women would be the first witnesses of Jesus' resurrection. Only Matthew notes that news of Jesus' miracle spread throughout the land (9.26). Both Mark and Luke record Jesus giving the parents strict orders not to spread the story (Mark 5.43; Luke

---

[57] France, *The Gospel of Matthew*, NICNT, 364.

[58] Witherington, *Women and the Genesis of Christianity*, 84.

[59] It seems to me that every resurrection story in the Jewish scriptures and Jesus' ministry points forward to His resurrection.

[60] France, *The Gospel of Matthew*, NICNT, 358 footnote 7 suggests the wording used to describe this resurrection points forward to how Jesus Himself will overcome death.

8.56), but Matthew does not record such a prohibition. As the book ends, the women are commanded to take the news of Jesus' resurrection to the disciples and are forbidden from keeping it to themselves (28.7, 10). In Matthew, resurrection is such good news it cannot be kept to oneself; it must be shared. This young lady is the first to have her life restored at the hands of Jesus, and women are the first to announce that all who follow Jesus will conquer death because of His resurrection.

4.10 Matthew 10.18

Jesus selects his twelve apostles (10.2–4) and sends them out on the limited commission to the nation of Israel (10.5–6).[61] He first warns that their message could be rejected and then moves toward harsher treatments they may experience for sharing the message of Jesus.[62] Jesus would stand before Jewish and Gentile authorities (Matt 26.57, 59; 27.2, 11),[63] and He prepares His followers to do the same. However, persecution will give an opportunity to share the message of Jesus with the Gentiles. While Matthew 10 focuses on the disciples' mission to Israel (10.5–6), it looks forward to the eventual mission to all nations.[64] Matthew looks past the limited commission of the Twelve to the Jews and provides a hint of the continuing mission of the church to all nations.[65]

4.11 Matthew 10.15; 11.20–24

John the Baptist and Jesus preach a message of repentance (3.2, 6, 8, 11; 4.17), yet the current generation rejects them both (11.16–19). Jesus' miracles were not performed to impress people but were calls to repentance (11.20).

---

[61] Please note 10.5–6 will be addressed later in chapter five.

[62] Craig L. Blomberg, *Matthew*, The New American Commentary, V.22 (Nashville: Broadman Press, 1992), 174.

[63] Turner, *Matthew*, BECNT, 276.

[64] Ibid, 276.

[65] Keener, *The Gospel of Matthew*, 323–324.

After speaking in general terms of His rejection (11.16–19), Jesus specifically calls out three towns: Chorazin, Bethsaida, and Capernaum. Chorazin and Bethsaida are near Capernaum at the northern end of the Sea of Galilee.[66] These two towns are not mentioned anywhere else in Matthew but witnessed a majority of Jesus miracles (11.20).[67] Capernaum is where Jesus settled and began His earthly ministry (4.13). Few others have an opportunity to witness as much evidence as Chorazin, Bethsaida, and Capernaum, yet it does not result in their repentance.[68]

If the pagan, prideful, idolatrous, immoral, and oppressive nations of Tyre, Sidon, and Sodom[69] could have witnessed Jesus' miraculous signs, they would have repented in tears and sackcloth! As a matter of fact, some in Tyre and Sidon who witness the signs of a prophet of God *did* repent (1 Kgs 17.9–24).[70] Those who reject Jesus (11.20–24) or the apostles' (10.15) miracles and message will experience greater wrath in judgment than these infamous nations. Sodom becomes a proverb of horror as it shows God's utter annihilation of wickedness (Dt 29.23), yet their sins are nothing in comparison to rejecting Jesus.[71]

In the gospel of Matthew, the reader has witnessed the Gentile Magi pay attention to the sign of the star while the Jews ignored it (2.1–12). The centurion knows Jesus possesses the power

---

[66] Turner, *Matthew*, BECNT, 299.

[67] Ibid, 300.

[68] Keener, *The Gospel of Matthew*, 345.

[69] For passages which list these characteristics of these three nations see Gen 18.16–19.29; 1 Kgs 16.31; Isa 23.1–17; Jer 25.22; 27.3–7; Ezek 16.49–50; 26.1–9; Joel 3:4–8; Zech 9.1–4.

[70] Craig S. Keener, *The IVP Bible Background Commentary: New Testament* (Downers Grover: IVP Academic, 1993), 77; also France, *The Gospel of Matthew*, NICNT, 438 who notes there is no mention of the impact Elijah had on anyone else in Tyre or Sidon other than the widow and her son.

[71] David E. Garland, *Reading Matthew: A Literary and Theological Commentary* (Macon: Smyth&Helwys Publishing Inc., 2001), 131.

to heal his servant from a distance because he knows Jesus possesses authority (8.5–13). Indeed, the Gentiles in Matthew have responded to the signs of Jesus while many Jews have not.

4.12 Matthew 12.18–21

Matthew emphasizes Jesus as the fulfillment of the Jewish Scriptures, and this is the longest quotation from the Scriptures in the book. While there is much to be gleaned from this quotation,[72] the reader should note the Servant's message proclaims peace and provides hope to Gentiles (12.18, 21). Isaiah 42 seems to have been a favorite passage of Jews and the early church to speak of outreach to the Gentiles. Simeon seems to quote from Isaiah 42.6 in Luke 2.32 when he describes Jesus' mission to his parents. Additionally, Paul quotes from Isaiah 42.6 in Acts 13.47 to state how they would

---

[72]This quote from Isaiah reveals much about Jesus identity. (1) Jesus is God's chosen Servant, (2) God is pleased with Him, (3) God's spirit rests on Him, (4) He proclaims justice for *all* people, and (5) he is gentle.

When an New Testament author quotes from the Jewish scriptures, they expect the reader to know the context of the quotation. Matthew leaves off his quotation in Isaiah 42.4, so what does the rest of Isaiah 42 tell us about this servant? Isaiah prophesied much about this coming servant (Isa 42.1; 49.7; 52.13) who will pay the ultimate price on behalf of the people. In Isaiah 42.4 this servant would bring a new law. He would be a savior to the Gentiles and covenant for all people (42.6). He would open the eyes of the blind and lead people out of prison (42.7). Because of the actions of the servant, we are called to sing a new song of praise to God (42.10–12) as God defeats all His enemies (42.13). Jesus will accomplish all these things!

Jesus will give his life for the sins of the people (Matt 1.21; connect with Isa 52.13–53.12; see also Matt. 8.17). Jesus ushered in a new law enacted on new and better promises (Heb 8.6). He opened the eyes of the blind and freed prisoners from the grasp of Satan (a fact Jesus will point out in 12.29). In Revelation we are called to sing a new song of praise to Jesus (Rev 5.9). Jesus came to defeat the greatest enemies of God's people: sin and death. Jesus is the fulfillment of the servant Isaiah spoke of, which points toward His rejection (Isa 42.18–25) and death on behalf of all people (Isa 52.13–53.12).

now take the Gospel to the Gentiles. When the Gentiles hear this news, they rejoice that eternal life is available to them (Acts 13.48).

In context, the religious leaders want to kill Jesus because he healed a man with a withered hand (12.9–14). This causes Jesus to withdraw, not wanting to stir up any premature confrontation and pointing to his gentle nature (12.20 quoting Isa 42.3). Large crowds follow him and he heals them but instructs them not to reveal his identity (12.15–16). Matthew interprets Jesus healing ministry and prohibition of announcing his identity as the fulfillment of Isaiah 42.1–4. Jesus' miracles, which were rejected by the Jewish leadership, point forward to Gentile inclusion. Since this is a fulfillment of the OT, the theme of Gentile inclusion is clearly rooted in the Jewish Scriptures.[73]

Since Jesus' ministry of healing points toward Gentile inclusion, the same line of reasoning can be applied to speak of the inclusion of women. Since Jesus heals many women (8.14–15; 9.18–26) it points toward their inclusion into his Kingdom.

4.13 Matthew 12.38–42

After Jesus rebukes the lack of insight the Pharisees' possess (12.24–37), they, along with the scribes, request a sign (once more showing a rejection of his miracles) to prove he is from God. Jesus states they crave a sign because they are an evil and adulterous generation (12.39), but they would only receive the sign of Jonah (12.39–40).[74]

Rather than grant a sign, Jesus informs the religious leaders there will be two key witnesses the prosecution will summon against this generation on the judgment day: the men of Nineveh and the Queen of the South. Jonah proclaims a mes-

---

[73] Keener, *The Gospel of Matthew*, 361; France, *The Gospel of Matthew*, NICNT, 472.

[74] The sign of Jonah seems to be a reference to the resurrection since Jonah's three days and nights in the fish is compared to the Son of Man's three days and nights in the heart of the earth.

sage of judgment (Jonah 3.4), never calls Nineveh to repent, and performs no sign, but the whole city fasts and repents in sackcloth (Jonah 3.5–10; note Matt 11.21). Jesus proclaims a message of hope (12.21; also 11.28–30), calls the people to repentance (4.17) and performs many signs (11.20).[75] He is greater than Jonah in every aspect, but this generation is more hardened than their ancient, pagan neighbors.

The Queen of the South takes the initiative to go to Solomon because she hears of His wisdom (1 Kgs 10.1–10). The Magi follow in her footsteps by coming from a great distance to seek one who is greater than Solomon (2.1–12), but this generation rejects the wisdom of Jesus.[76] Thus, both male and female Gentiles serve as a positive example of how one ought to respond to the teaching of the Gospel.

4.14 Matthew 12.46–50

The doubts of the religious leaders seem to be shared, to some degree, by Jesus' family.[77] When His mother and brothers request His presence outside, away from the crowds, Jesus responds by stating His mother, brothers, and sisters are those who hear and obey the will of God.

Once more, women are included and viewed as close relatives of Jesus. In Jesus' description of the family of God there is no mention of "fathers" but only mothers, brothers, and sisters. There is only One Father, and all men and women serve equally under His authority.[78] Jesus often uses family language to describe his

---

[75] Garland, *Reading Matthew*, 142.

[76] France, *The Gospel of Matthew*, NICNT, 76, 492–493; Keener, *The Gospel of Matthew*, 368.

[77] Keener, *The Gospel of Matthew*, 369 who states the parallel account in Mark 3.20–35 brackets Jesus family's concerns (Mark 3.20–21, 31–35) with the Pharisee's accusation that Jesus was working with the devil (Mark 3.22–30).

[78] F. S. Spencer. "Women" in *DJG*, 1005.

followers. As was seen previously, when Jesus heals the woman who was suffering from with a hemorrhaging for twelve years, he calls her "daughter" (9.22). This is how Jesus refers to her in all the parallel accounts (Mark 5.34; Luke 8.48) and it is the only time in the gospels that he refers to a woman as daughter.[79] She heeds the will of the Father and becomes a child of Jesus. At the resurrection, Jesus instructs the women to take word to "my brethren" (28.10). In Jesus' unique role as fully human and fully divine, he sees himself as father and brother to those who obey his word. Anyone can become part of the family of Jesus if we imitate the example of the sick woman and heed the words of our Master and Brother.

4.15 Matthew 13

Matthew 13 is almost entirely devoted to Jesus teaching the crowds in parables (13.34–35) and explaining the parables to His disciples (13.10–23, 36–43). [80] The parables hold a wealth of teaching about the Kingdom of God, but our focus will be on references to Gentiles and women.[81] Jesus' parables are so inclusive that no gender or race is excluded from the implications of His teaching.[82]

4.15.1 Matthew 13.31–32

The parable of the mustard seed and yeast both point forward to massive expansion of the Kingdom of God with an eye to

---

[79] The closest parallel would be Luke 13.16 where he refers to a woman who had been bent double for 18 years as a "daughter of Abraham." However, this is not parallel to calling this woman daughter.

[80] For more on this chapter revealing Gentile inclusion see Terry R. Baughman, "Gentile Inclusion in the Kingdom of Heaven as Revealed in Matthew 13" (Master's Thesis, Western Seminary, 1999), 65–112.

[81] For more on the interpretation of the parables see Craig L. Blomberg, *Interpreting the Parables*. 2nd ed. (Downers Grove: IVP Academic, 2012).

[82] Robert Farrar Capon, *The Parables of the Kingdom* (Grand Rapids: Eerdmans Publishing Company, 1985), 73.

the inclusion of the Gentiles and women. The mustard seed is planted by a man, presumably a farmer, and it grows into a massive tree,[83] able to provide a home for the birds of the air. Jewish teachers often use the birds as symbols of a universal coming kingdom while the Jewish Scriptures often use the birds to describe the Gentile nations (Ezek 17.22–23; 31.5–6; Dan 4.12, 21).[84] The imagery of the birds nesting in the branches implies the kingdom of heaven will grow until it encompasses the entire world.[85] A Jewish audience would not miss the implication of the birds.[86]

4.15.2 Matthew 13.33

The parable of leaven parallels the previous parable of the mustard seed. While the mustard seed is planted by a male farmer (13.31), here we see a woman laboring in the household to make bread. Engaged in the preparation of a meal for her family, this woman's work serves as an illustration of how quickly God's kingdom will spread.[87] Jesus may have told these two parables together not merely because they prove a similar point, but to emphasize the gospel was for men and women. Each engaged in their traditional roles and they each serve as productive examples of analogy for his work.[88]

---

[83] France, *The Gospel of Matthew*, NICNT, 527 suggested 12.32 could be a quote from Daniel 4.12 to draw a "comparison between the great but short-lived earthly empire of Babylon and the far greater and more permanent kingdom of heaven."

[84] Baughman, "Gentile Inclusion in the Kingdom of Heaven as Revealed in Matthew 13" M.A. Thesis, 80; see also Garland, *Reading Matthew*, 151.

[85] Baughman, "Gentile Inclusion in the Kingdom of Heaven as Revealed in Matthew 13" M.A. Thesis, 80.

[86] Ibid, 87.

[87] F. S. Spencer. "Women" in *DJG*, 1006.

[88] Witherington, *Women and the Genesis of Christianity*, 56.

4.15.3 Matthew 13.24–30, 36–43

The parable of the wheat and tares is given (13.24–30) and explained privately to the disciples (13.36–43). Clearly the parable speaks of the final judgment and the reward or judgment which awaits everyone. Jesus explains every aspect of the parable (13.37–39) and informs the disciples, "the field is the world" (13.38). The implication is that the sons of the kingdom will encompass all parts of the globe.[89]

4.16 Matthew 15.21–28

Due to the negative elements of Jesus ignoring this woman's first request, the disciples' request to send her away, Jesus' statement concerning his mission directed toward Israel, and the insulting slang term he uses for Gentiles, this passage will also be discussed later in section five. For now, our focus will rest on the positive aspects of this story.

After the Pharisees challenge Jesus concerning hand washing, he and his disciples withdraw to Tyre and Sidon (15.21). This passage reinforces a Matthean invitation of the Gentile mission and reminds the reader how Tyre and Sidon are open to repentance while Chorazin and Bethsaida are not (11.20–22).[90] This Canaanite woman will not be turned away despite the initial rebuff by both Jesus and His disciples (15.23–24). She wants healing for her daughter, who was "cruelly demon-possessed" (15.22), and firmly believes Jesus can help her. A temple dedicated to Eshmun, a god of healing, is located nearby[91] but the woman seeks *Jesus*, not Esh-

---

[89]While Wilkins, *Matthew*, NIV Application Commentary, 485 agrees with this, France, *The Gospel of Matthew*, NICNT, 535 sees this just as a generic reference to people and not a passage which speaks of Gentile inclusion. However, if the term simply means "people" then that implies all people will be subject to the judgment of Jesus (25.32). Therefore, if all will be judged by Jesus, then certainly all are welcome into His Kingdom.

[90]Keener, *The Gospel of Matthew*, 415.

[91]Wilkins, *Matthew*, NIV Application Commentary, 539

mun, for healing. While Mark describes her as a "Gentile, of the Syrophoenician race" (Mark 7.26), Matthew calls her a Canaanite (15.22). Matthew alters his description of this woman to present her not merely as a Gentile but as a traditional enemy of Israel.[92]

This Canaanite woman's request stands in stark contrast with other people in the gospel. The religious leaders *want* a sign from Jesus (12.38). Herod *wants* John the Baptist dead (14.5). James and John *want* positions of power in Jesus' kingdom (20.20–23). Judas *wants* money (26.15) and the crowds *want* Barabbas (27.15, 17, 21). This woman simply *wants* healing for her daughter.[93]

The Canaanite woman's faith stands in contrast with the disciples and in line with the other Gentiles and women in Matthew. This is the second time in Matthew Jesus said someone possessed "great" faith (8.10).[94] In contrast, the disciples (8.26), and specifically Peter (14.28–31), were said to possess "little faith."[95] In Matthew, Jesus praises three people for their faith: a Gentile centurion (8.10–13), a woman who was afflicted with a hemorrhage for twelve years (9.22), and a Canaanite woman (15.28). This woman serves as a reminder that entry into Jesus' kingdom is not based on being Jewish or male, but on faith.[96]

4.17 Matthew 15.29–39

After healing the Canaanite woman's daughter, Jesus goes "by the Sea of Galilee" (15.29) and ascends a mountain.[97] The crowds

---

[92]Melanie S. Baffes, "Jesus and the Canaanite Woman: A story of Reversal" *Journal of Theta Alpha Kappa* 35 no. 2 (2011): 12–23.

[93]Garland, *Reading Matthew*, 166.

[94]France, *The Gospel of Matthew*, NICNT, 595–596 states this is the only time great qualifies faith but he seems to overlook 8.10.

[95]Witherington, *Women and the Genesis of Christianity*, 76; France, *The Gospel of Matthew*, NICNT, 596.

[96]Melanie S. Baffes, "Jesus and the Canaanite Woman: A story of Reversal" *Journal of Theta Alpha Kappa* 35 no. 2 (2011): 12–23.

[97]Many significant things happen to Jesus while He is on a mountain in the book of Matthew (4.8–10; 5.1; 15.29; 17.1; 28.16).

flock to Him, so Jesus heals and, for the second time in Matthew (14.13–21), feeds them. While some have seen Jesus' second feeding miracle as designed to portray him as the ultimate fulfillment of the Jewish Scriptures,[98] many argue the entire section of 15.21–38 is Jesus ministering to Gentiles.[99]

Hilary of Poitiers (c. 315–367) is the first known church father to declare the ethnic makeup of the people Jesus healed and fed in the feeding of four thousand to be Gentile.[100] Hilary argues the context points in this direction. Jesus has just healed a little Canaanite girl from the grip of Satan and in the following account He goes to a Gentile community and heals their sick so they might "be freed like the girl from any power of the unclean spirits."[101] Others contend that the Gentile mother receiving "crumbs" under the table signals to the reader the following miracle of feeding the 4,000 took place in Gentile territory and foresees Gentile inclusion.[102]

Several have continued to build upon the arguments of Hilary of Poitiers citing geography and literary hints as proof this mira-

---

[98]Turner, *Matthew*, BECNT, 392–394, who argues Moses (Ex. 16; Num. 11), Elijah (1 Kgs 17.3–6, 8–16), and Elisha (2 Kgs 4.1–7, 38–44) all preformed two feeding miracles, so it would be natural for Matthew, who focused on Jesus fulfilling the Jewish scriptures, to include two feeding miracles of Jesus. He also sees this account as emphasizing Jesus compassion and both feeding miracles as seeking to build the disciple's faith. See also Keener, *The Gospel of Matthew*, 418–419.

[99]France, *The Gospel of Matthew*, NICNT, 597. See also Carson, "Matthew" in *EBC*, 356–359; Blomberg, *Matthew*, 245; Chumbley, *The Gospel of Matthew*, 289.

[100]J. R. C. Cousland, "The Feeding of the Four Thousand Gentiles in Matthew? Matthew 15.29–39 as a Test Case," *Novum Testamentum* 41, no.1 (1999), 1–23.

[101]Manlio Simonetti, *Ancient Christian Commentary on Scripture: Matthew 14–28*, Vol. 1b (Downers Grove: InterVarsity Press, 2002), 33.

[102]Wilkins, *Matthew*, NIV Application Commentary, 541.

cle was done for a Gentile audience. First, it is argued Matthew's lack of geographical statement must assume he places this event in the Decapolis, like Mark does (Mark 7.31), which had a high Gentile population. Jesus' next stop is the "region of Magadan" (15.39), a location unknown today, but which must have been Jewish territory, because he is greeted by Pharisees and Sadducees in the next account (16.1).

Second, others argue in the Jewish Scriptures, the use of the phrase "God of Israel" (15.31) is found on the lips of those outside Israel (1 Sam 5.7–8, 10–11; 6.3, 5).[103] D. A. Carson says, "The phrase 'they glorified the God of Israel' (15.31) could be naturally said only by Gentiles."[104] R.T. France argues, "This is never said about the Galilean crowds, and the terminology suggests that the crowds are Gentiles, recognizing the special power of the Jewish Messiah."[105]

Third, and lastly, the different Greek words to describe the basket are viewed as significant. The Greek word for "basket" in 14.20 (Gk. *kophinos*) is a Jewish term but in 15.37 the Greek word (Gk. *spuris*) is a Hellenistic term[106] which serves as a "minor pointer to a different cultural setting for the two [feedings]."[107] These and several other lines of argumentation see 15.29–39 as providing an answer to 15.21–28 and showing there is an adequate amount of "crumbs" for the Gentiles. Ultimately, they will not have to settle for crumbs but will be seated at the table for the Messianic Feast (8.11–12).

While at first these arguments might seem convincing, this interpretation is debated. From Matthew, there is inadequate

---

[103] Cousland, "The Feeding of the Four Thousand Gentiles in Matthew," 8.

[104] Carson, "Matthew" in *EBC*, 357.

[105] France, *The Gospel of Matthew*, NICNT, 597.

[106] France, *The Gospel of Matthew*, NICNT, 603 and Blomberg, *Matthew*, 245.

[107] France, *The Gospel of Matthew*, NICNT, 603.

geographical data to be certain where this event took place.[108] Matthew could have employed a different term for basket not to imply an ethnic statement, but to show the abundance of left-overs.[109] The strongest argument for 15.29–39 taking place in a Gentile region rests on the phrase "glorified the God of Israel" (15.31), but this argument is not as convincing as it might at first appear.

As noted above, it is certainly possible for this phrase to be found on the lips of Gentiles, but the phrase often appears on the lips of Jews in the Jewish Scriptures (Ex 5.1; Josh 7.19–20; 9.19; 24.23; 1 Sam 1.17; 20.2; 1 Kgs 1.48; 1 Chron 16.36; Pss 41.13; 59.5; 68.35; 69.6; 72.18; 106.48; Isa 24.15; 29.23; 37.16) and in the New Testament (Luke 1.68; see also Acts 13.17).[110] As a matter of fact, almost 95 percent of the uses of "God of Israel," and its variants, in the Jewish Scriptures are attributed to Jews.[111]

Matthew's larger use of the terms "Israel" and "Jews" could shed light on the makeup of this crowd. Every time a Gentile speaks in Matthew, they use the term Jews rather than Israel. When the Magi come they want to know where they can find the "King of the Jews" (2.2). Pilate asks Jesus if He is the "King of the Jews" (27.11) and writes "King of the Jews" as the charge above Jesus' head (27.37). The Roman soldiers mocked Jesus as the "King of the Jews" (27.29) while the chief priests, scribes and

---

[108] Cousland, "The Feeding of the Four Thousand Gentiles in Matthew," 14.

[109] This will be discussed later in the paper, but the word translated basket in 15.37 is a much larger basket used to collect the leftovers after the feeding of the 5,000 (14.20).

[110] Turner, *Matthew*, BECNT, 392–393 and Jack P. Lewis, *The Gospel According to Matthew, Part 2: 13.53–28.20* (Austin: Sweet Publishing Company, 1976), 30.

[111] Cousland, "The Feeding of the Four Thousand Gentiles in Matthew," 18.

elders mock His claim to be the "King of Israel" (27.41–42).[112] Thus, while it is possible that Jesus heals and feeds an all-Gentile crowd, the evidence does not seem to point this direction. However, this in no way diminishes Jesus' inclusion of Gentiles in the gospel of Matthew.

4.18 Matthew 16.13–20

Peter's confession shows the disciples are starting to understand Jesus' identity (15.16; 16.11–12),[113] but do not yet have a full understanding of His mission (16.21–28). It shows God is revealing information to the disciples and challenges people not to merely adopt what others believe about Jesus but to make a personal decision (16.13–16).

While much debate centers around this passage, our focus rests on the place where Peter makes his confession: the district of Caesarea Philippi. This location is about twenty-five miles north of the Sea of Galilee.[114] While both Jews and Gentiles live there (Josephus, *Life* 13.74),[115] it is predominantly a Gentile region.[116] The city was built by Philip the tetrarch and named to honor Caesar Augustus and himself.[117] This region had long engaged in the worship of Baal and at that time contained a cave which was turned into a shrine to honor the Greek god Pan.[118] It is in this

---

[112] An examination of who uses the term "Israel" in Matthew would yield the conclusion that "Israel" is a term used by those who were Jewish in the Gospel (2.6, 20–21; 8.10; 9.33; 10.6, 23; 15.24; 19.28; 27.9, 42).

[113] The theme of "understanding" is important in Matthew. It separates the disciple from the non-disciple (13.19, 23, 51; 15.16; 16.11–12).

[114] Turner, *Matthew*, BECNT, 403 and Keener, *The Gospel of Matthew*, 424.

[115] Lewis, *The Gospel of Matthew, Part 2: 13.53–28.20*, 35.

[116] Wilkins, *Matthew*, NIV Application Commentary, 557 and Garland, *Reading Matthew*, 171.

[117] Lewis, *The Gospel of Matthew, Part 2: 13.53–28.20*, 35.

[118] Wilkins, *Matthew*, NIV Application Commentary, 557; Turner,

Gentile-filled, pagan center of worship that Peter makes the great confession which is revealed to him by the Heavenly Father.[119] The location of Peter's great confession seems to foreshadow the scope of the great commission.

4.19 Matthew 18.1–6

Jesus welcoming outcasts has been epitomized by Gentiles and women, but now we encounter another lowly group in Matthew 18–19 that Jesus receives warmly: children. Interestingly, Hilary of Poitiers interprets Jesus welcoming the children in 19.13–15 allegorically as pointing toward Gentile inclusion.[120]

Children were certainly at the bottom of the social ladder. Mortality rate was extremely high for children in the ancient world[121] which is attested to in the gospels by the number of parents who request Jesus to heal their sick child. Roman parents had the legal right to abandon their child in a public space for

---

Matthew, BECNT, 403. See also Lewis, *The Gospel of Matthew, Part 2: 13.53–28.20*, 35.

[119] Keener, *The Gospel of Matthew*, 424.

[120] Hilary of Poitiers commenting on Matthew 19:13, quote found in Manlio Simonetti (Ed.), *Ancient Christian Commentary on Scripture: Matthew 14–28*, New Testament 1b (Downers Grove: InterVarsity Press, 2001), 95:

The children prefigure the Gentiles, to whom salvation is given through faith and the simple word. But since the goal was first to save Israel, they were at first prevented by the disciples from approaching. The action of the apostles is not about their personal desires but rather their serving as a type or prefiguring of the future proclamation of the gospel to the Gentiles. The Lord says that the children should not be prevented because "theirs is the kingdom of heaven"; for the grace and gift of the Holy Spirit was going to be bestowed on the Gentiles by the laying on of hands, when the work of the law ceased.

[121] C. Reeder, "Child, Children" in *Dictionary of Jesus and the Gospels*, 2nd Edition. Editors Joel B. Green, Jeannine K. Brown, & Nicholas Perrin (Downers Grove: IVP Academic, 2013), 109–113 suggests that only 50 percent of children survived past the age of ten.

others to raise as their own or expose the child to the elements to die. If the parents were poor or the child was handicap or female the odds of exposure increased. Jews did not practice exposing their children (Josephus, *Against Apion* 2.202). Often the quality of a child's life would be dependent on the social status of the family that the child was born into. Wealthy families were able to provide toys and a good education for their children while in poorer families the children began working long hours at an early age to assist in providing for the family.[122]

While there should not be an attempt to romanticize ancient people's attitude toward children, we should also be careful not to overstate their mistreatment. Children could be taken advantage of, had no status or rights, and many were impatient toward them. However, it does seem the tide was shifting in favor of viewing children more positively. Many ancient philosophers viewed them as innocent and future productive members of society.[123] Jews would have viewed children as gifts from God (Dt 28.4; Pss 127.3–5; 128.3–4). As mentioned above, the fact that both Jew and Gentile parents come to Jesus requesting him to heal their children shows they saw great value in their children (9.18–31; 15.21–28; 17.14–18).

In Matthew 18, the disciples want to know who is the greatest and Jesus uses a child as a visual aid. He calls them to have the humility of a child (18.4), which in this context, seems to refer to realizing their dependence on God like children realize their dependence on their parents. Additionally, they must be willing to receive someone who has such low social status (18.5).

As Jesus begins to instruct his disciples about greatness Jesus "calls" (Gk. proskaleomai) a child to him. Matthew employs the same Greek verb (Gk. proskaleomai) when Jesus "calls" the disci-

---

[122]C. Reeder, "Child, Children" in *Dictionary of Jesus and the Gospels*, 109–113.

[123]Warren Carter, *Households and Discipleship: A Study of Matthew 19–20* (England: JOST Press, 1994), 95–113.

ples (10.1; see also 10.2–4). Children serve as a model for the true disciple to imitate.[124] The path to greatness in Jesus' kingdom lies in humility and receiving the least of all.

4.20 Matthew 19.13–15

Parents begin to bring their small children to Jesus so that he might place his hands on them and pray. However, when the disciples see this, they rebuke them and attempt to keep the children away from Jesus. They assume Jesus is much too busy and important to be bothered by children. However, Jesus informs the disciples the children are to be welcomed (see also 18.5) "for the kingdom of heaven belongs to such as these" (19.14).

The following story of the man, who is commonly referred to as the rich young ruler, stands in strong contrast to Jesus receiving the children. The man is concerned about eternal life (19.16) and has been a faithful follower of God's Law (19.18–20). His wealth (19.22) would have been viewed as a gift from God due to his righteousness. Yet, when he refuses to part with his wealth, Jesus tells his disciples it is difficult for a "rich man to enter the kingdom of heaven" (19.23). The disciples are astonished at the statement and wonder if any can be saved (19.25). While Jesus answers their immediate question by reminding them that salvation is only possible with God (19.26), he has already answered the question in the previous account. To receive eternal life, one must become like a child (19.14; see also 18.4–5).

4.21 Matthew 21.12–16

Jesus enters Jerusalem riding on a donkey in fulfillment of Zechariah 9.9 and to the joy of the crowd who accompanied Him. Jerusalem is "stirred" (21.10) and inquires about the identity of this individual. Jesus' first action after entering Jerusalem is to cleanse the temple by driving out the money changers and illustrating that their use of the temple is in violation of the Scriptures.

---

[124]Carter, *Households and Discipleship*, 96.

It is logical to assume the buying, selling, and exchanging of money is taking place in the "Court of the Gentiles."[125] If this is true, then one issue which bothered Jesus is taking away the one place in the temple the Gentiles were welcomed. This might explain why Jesus quotes from Isaiah 56.7[126] while driving out the vendors. Isaiah 56 speaks of the inclusion of outcasts such as eunuchs (56.1–5). It looks forward to the day when the Gentiles will be included in the people of God. "Also the foreigners who join themselves to the LORD, to minister to Him, and to love the name of the LORD, to be His servants, everyone who keeps from profaning the sabbath and holds fast My covenant…" (Isa 56.6). Isaiah 56.7, the verse which Jesus quoted from, states the temple was a "house of prayer for *all the peoples.*"

Jesus' inclusion of outcasts seems to continue in the next verse as the blind and lame come for healing in the temple (21.14). Jesus heals and welcomes the blind and lame, who had traditionally been prevented from obtaining access to God's presence (Lev 21.18–19; see also 2 Sam 5.8; 11QTemple 45.13; *Mishna Hagiga* 1.1).[127] Jesus longs for current outcasts to be included in his kingdom.

The religious leaders see all the "wonderful" things Jesus did (21.15) but are outraged that the children are shouting, "Hosanna to the son of David." They demand that Jesus quiet his young supporters, but Jesus refuses. Instead, Jesus informs the religious leaders that the children are fulfilling scripture by praising him. The children recognize Jesus' identity and praise him for his mira-

---

[125]Turner, *Matthew*, BECNT, 499; Wilkins, *Matthew*, NIV Application Commentary, 691–692; Keener, *The Gospel of Matthew*, 499–500. France, *The Gospel of Matthew*, NICNT, 787 in footnote 19 reminds the reader the "Court of the Gentiles" is the modern name given to the area where Gentiles were confined. Of course, Jews were allowed in this part of the temple, but Gentiles could not go any further.

[126]The quote in 21.13 is a combination of Isaiah 56.7 and Jeremiah 7.11.

[127]Garland, *Reading Matthew*, 216.

cles, while the religious leaders remain blind. The religious leaders must become like children for their eyes to be opened.

4.22 Matthew 21.43

Jesus has just related a parable which plays heavily off of Isaiah 5.1–7. Jesus shows there is a consistent thread that has run through Jewish history that God's chosen nation has, sadly, always rejected God's messengers. For their rebellious actions they would receive judgment. While at first it appears 21.43 seems to view the Gentiles replacing the Jews as the people of God, on closer observation that view seems to be mistaken.[128] The reader is informed explicitly in 21.45 that the parable is told as a rebuke of the Jewish religious leaders. The Jewish leaders might have failed but any Jew or Gentile who produces fruit are welcome (3.8; 7.15–20; 12.33; 21.18–22)! Furthermore, the exclusion of Jews would not fit Matthew's theology of all being welcomed. Gentile inclusion does not require Jewish exclusion. Matthew's point all along has been that all are welcome, and space is not limited!

4.23 Matthew 24.14

Jesus privately answers several questions the disciples have about the destruction of Jerusalem, His final coming, and the end of the world (24.3). For space reasons, a complete examination of Matthew 24 is not possible, but it should be noted that 24.4–35 discusses the destruction of Jerusalem. Jesus predicts all the events of 24.4–35 will take place in the life of His disciples (24.34).

Amid His predictions about the destruction of Jerusalem, Jesus predicts the gospel will be preached throughout the *"whole world* as a testimony to *all the nations...*" (24.14). Jesus prophesies the gospel will become a worldwide phenomenon in a short time.[129] Persecution will result in the spread of the gospel (24.9–

---

[128] Turner, *Matthew*, BECNT, 517.

[129] Paul stated the gospel had spread to (Rom 16.26; Col 1.23) and borne fruit in the entire world (Col 1.6).

14).[130] This verse anticipates Jesus' final instruction of the great commission to His followers.[131]

4.24 Matthew 25.32

The previous parable tells how three slaves are called to give an account to their master (25.14–30). The following account (25.31–46) informs the reader all nations will give an account before Jesus (25.32). Matthew's use of the phrase "all nations" always refers to the entire world which the disciples are called to evangelize (24.9, 14; 28.19).[132]

In the Jewish Scriptures, God sits upon His throne and gathers the nations for judgment based on how they treated His people (Dan 7.9–12; Joel 3.1–17). Jewish literature looks forward to the same idea (4 Ezra 7.37).[133] In Matthew 25, Jesus sits upon the throne and all people (Jews and Gentiles) must give an account based on how they have treated the family of Jesus.[134] If the message of Jesus is universal, so, also, must be the judgment.

4.25 Matthew 26.6–13

Matthew's Passion narrative begins by Jesus reminding His disciples that His death, which He predicted many times (16.21; 17.22–23; 20.17–19), is only two days away (26.1–2). The chief priests plot to kill Jesus (26.3–5) and Judas agrees to assist them in their endeavor in exchange for thirty pieces of silver (26.14–16). In the middle of these two passages, the reader encounters an unnamed woman (26.6–13).

While women have always been present in Jesus' ministry (27.55), in the final chapters of Matthew, women escape from

---

[130] Garland, *Reading Matthew*, 242; France, *The Gospel of Matthew*, NICNT, 908; Keener, *The Gospel of Matthew*, 572.

[131] Garland, *Reading Matthew*, 242.

[132] Ibid, 247.

[133] Keener, *The Gospel of Matthew*, 603.

[134] Garland, *Reading Matthew*, 248.

the margins and become the key characters of the story.[135] The women in the Passion narrative will provide an example of the devotion and insight which all followers of Jesus must imitate.

An unnamed woman approaches Jesus as he dines in the home of Simon the leper and pours a "very costly perfume" (26.7) on His head. This pricey perfume could have been nard, an imported ointment from the east (Hor. *Ode.* 2.11.16) and was perhaps an heirloom which had been handed down from past generations.[136] This woman is willing to spend a fortune to anoint Jesus while "Judas, one of the twelve," (26.14) is willing to betray Jesus for a measly thirty pieces of silver (26.15).

The woman anointing Jesus' head, rather than washing His feet, was probably symbolic. In the Jewish Scriptures, three groups were anointed: prophets (1 Kgs 19.16), priests (Ex 29.21; Lev 8.30), and kings (1 Sam 10.1; 16.12–13; 1 Kgs 19.16; 2 Kgs 9.3). Jesus is in the unique position to be all three. He is a prophet (13.57; 26.21, 26, 31, 34, 47–50, 56, 75) who serves as believers' great High Priest (Heb 5–10), and is King of Kings (25.34, 40; see also Luke 1.32–33).[137]

However, anointing was not simply meant to inaugurate one to an office but was generally administered by a command of God to mark the person for their divinely appointed task (Lev 8.30; 1 Sam 10.1; 16.1–13).[138] Jesus has been chosen by God to serve man through his suffering (Matt. 20.28) and ultimately, this woman anoints Jesus' body for burial (26.12). She emerges as the lone figure in Matthew who accepts and grasps Jesus' prophecies of His death. She alone is granted the honor

---

[135] Sheila E. McGinn, "Why now the Women? Social-Historical Insights on Gender Roles in Matthew 26–28" *Proceedings EGL & MWBS* 17 (1997): 107–114.

[136] Keener, *The Gospel of Matthew*, 618.

[137] Matthew's use of "Son of David" (1.1; 9.27; 12.23; 15.22; 20.30–31; 21.15; 22.42) also seems to point to Jesus' rightful position as King.

[138] France, *The Gospel of Matthew*, NICNT, 974.

of anointing Jesus' body for death since the women who went to the tomb on the first day of the week found it empty.[139] This woman shows insight the disciples lacked.[140] When Jesus first informs the disciples His path will lead to the cross (16.21), Peter rebukes Him, telling him that would never happen (16.22). This woman not only realizes Jesus' identity and His fulfillment of offices in the Jewish Scriptures but prepares him for His burial. She, in contrast to Peter, had in mind God's interest, not man's (16.23).

The disciples become angry with the woman and accuse her of being wasteful because they think she fails to give to the poor. They are considering the cost of the perfume; the woman considers the cost Jesus will pay for the sins of the world. Jesus dismisses their complaints by declaring the woman has done a "good deed" (26.10; Gk. *kalos ergon*). This is the same two Greek words Jesus uses in 5.16 when he calls His followers to be light to the world by engaging in "good deeds" (Gk. *kalos ergon*) to bring glory to their Father in heaven.[141] This unnamed woman serves as an example to all future generations of how to be a light to the world.[142]

Far from rebuking her, Jesus elevates her in front of the disciples by saying, "Truly I say to you, wherever this gospel is preached in the whole world, what this woman has done will also be spoken of in memory of her" (26.13). Jesus, again, envisions the gospel spreading to the entire world and this woman serves as the prime example of discipleship. Once more, 26.13 combines the

---

[139] F. S. Spencer. "Women" in *DJG*, 1006–1007.

[140] Dorothy Jean Weaver, "'Wherever This Good News is Proclaimed': Women and God in the Gospel of Matthew," *Interpretation* 64, no 4 (2010), 390–401.

[141] Stuart Love, *Jesus and Marginal Women: The Gospel of Matthew in Social-Scientific Perspective* (Eugene: Cascade Books, 2009), 182.

[142] The reader will recall the universal message in 5.13–16, as presented in that context.

themes of Gentile and women inclusion. Hilary of Poitiers ties our two themes together when he says, "This woman prefigures the Gentile people, who gave glory to God in the suffering of Christ."[143] James and John request to be given positions of honor in Jesus' Kingdom, but Jesus tells the disciples the path to greatness lies in serving others (20.26–27). He came to serve, and he expects that same heart in his followers (20.28). This woman is an amazing example of one who sets out to serve and is honored with being great in the Kingdom!

The context must be noted to highlight Matthew's praise of this woman. This is the fourth and final time that Jesus predicts His upcoming death (26.1–2). The first three are recorded in 16.21; 17.22–23; and 20.17–19. When Jesus first predicts His death (16.21), Peter rebukes him. After Jesus' second prediction of death the disciples are saddened (17.22–23), but then inquire about who is the greatest in the kingdom (18.1). The third time (20.17–19), James and John follow His prediction of death with a request for positions of honor and power in His coming kingdom (20.20–23). After each prediction of death, the disciples respond inappropriately.

With the fourth prediction of His death (26.1–2), the disciples' response is not recorded by Matthew. The scene shifts to those who plot Jesus' death (26.3–5) and then back to Jesus dining at the home of Simon the leper (26.6–13). Based on the structure of prediction and the disciples' response in the previous three occasions, perhaps the reader is to view the actions of the woman as a disciple's proper response to Jesus' prediction of His death. That is certainly how Jesus views it (26.12)! Thus, the woman is contrasted with the twelve. Their responses betray their thinking (16.23; 20.20–28), but the woman was the only one to respond appropriately to Jesus' prediction of death.

---

[143] Simonetti, *Ancient Christian Commentary on Scripture: Matthew 14–28*, 240.

4.26 Matthew 27.19

This verse is unique to Matthew.[144] Pilate's wife lends her voice to the chorus of people declaring Jesus to be innocent (27.4, 18, 23). Pilate knows Jesus is innocent but will not listen to the voice of his wife. Instead, he heeds the words of the crowds who call for Jesus' death (27.22–26). Augustine contrasts Pilate's wife with Eve. Eve incites her husband to commit a sin which leads to death, while Pilate's wife tries to persuade her husband to grant life to Jesus.[145] Her warning to release Jesus is contrasted with Pilate's willingness to surrender Jesus to the whims of the blood-thirsty crowd.[146] Pilate, knowing Jesus is innocent, seeks to remove himself from the guilt of the situation by washing his hands and placing the blame on the Jewish crowd (27.24).[147]

Pilate's wife realizes Jesus is a "righteous man." This is the second woman in the Passion narrative to possess insight about Jesus.[148] Her attempts to intervene highlight the religious leader's guilt. She is motivated to speak up for Jesus because she desires to see justice administered while the chief priest desires Jesus' death out of envy (27.18, 20). In contrast to the religious leaders, this woman has not witnessed Jesus' "wonderful" miracles (21.15) or been present to

---

[144]For a good article on this verse see Florence Morgan Gillman, "The Wife of Pilate (Matthew 27.19)," *Louvain Studies* 17 (1992): 152–165. Gillman covers a host of issues and has compiled some wonderful thoughts.

[145]Raymond E. Brown, *The Death of the Messiah: From Gethsemane to the Grave*, Vol. 1 (New York: Doubleday, 1994), 804.

[146]Jack Dean Kingsbury, *Matthew as Story*, 2nd Edition (Philadelphia: Fortress Press, 1988) 27.

[147]Daniel J. Hanlon, "The Function of the Gentile Characters in the Gospel of Matthew" (Master Thesis, Trinity Evangelical Divinity School, 2010), 148, 154 thinks Pilate's wife was acting out of concern for her husband rather than Jesus. He sees Pilate's reluctance to sentence Jesus directly tied to his wife's warning. The same line of thought is followed by Brown, *The Death of the Messiah*, 806.

[148]Garland, *Reading Matthew*, 261.

listen to His wisdom (21.45–46; 22.15–46) but had a dream which convinced her of Jesus' innocence and righteousness.[149] Pilate's wife pleads on Jesus' behalf (27.19) while the religious leaders stir up the crowd to request the release of Barabbas.[150]

While some in church history have viewed Pilate's wife as a believer and even made her a saint, Matthew does not mention or imply she became a follower of Christ.[151] It is intriguing that while Matthew did not call her a disciple he said she "suffered greatly" (27.19) because of Jesus, which is what he calls his followers to do (10.16–23; 16.24–28; 24.9–22).[152] However the main point for us is that Matthew's Passion Narrative continues to portray women very positively.

The modern reader might quickly dismiss the dream of Pilate's wife as a pagan omen,[153] but dreams were viewed as significant and prophetic in the ancient world.[154] In the Jewish Scriptures, Gentiles had dreams which were said to be revelations from Yahweh (Gen 20.3–7; 40.5–23; 41.25, 28, 32; Dan 2.28; 4.5, 19–27). In the gospel of Matthew, dreams played a big role in Jesus' birth narrative. Interestingly, dreams directed Joseph, a righteous Jew (1.19–25; 2.13–14, 19–21, 22), the Gentile Magi (2.12), and a Gentile woman (27.19). Her dream is linked with the previous ones in Matthew and seen as divinely given.[155]

---

[149] France, *Matthew*, NICNT, 1055.

[150] Gillman, "The Wife of Pilate (Matthew 27.19)," 155–156.

[151] Brown, *The Death of the Messiah*, Vol. 1, 804. It is interesting that in church history, most viewed Pilate's wife very positively, even making her a saint. However, there were some who argued her dream was from the devil because if she had been successful in convincing her husband to release Jesus then the world would not have received salvation.

[152] Weaver, "'Wherever This Good News is Proclaimed': Women and God in the Gospel of Matthew," *Interpretation*, 400.

[153] Wilkins, *Matthew*, NIV Application Commentary, 875.

[154] Turner, *Matthew*, BECNT, 653; France, *Matthew*, NICNT, 1055.

[155] Daniel J. Hanlon, "The Function of the Gentile Characters in the Gospel of Matthew," M.A. Thesis, Trinity Evangelical Divinity School,

God was willing to send a message via a dream regardless of race and gender.[156]

4.27 Matthew 27.45–56

As Jesus dies on the cross, the only people around him are Roman soldiers and the onlookers who mock Him. For three hours during the middle of the day, darkness covers the sky as Jesus hangs on the cross. As Jesus breathes his last, an earthquake occurs, the veil of the temple is ripped in half, and some "saints" who had died are raised from the dead (27.50–53).

The centurion and those with him had probably witnessed multiple crucifixions. It is likely they are present for the scourging (27.26) and perhaps have participated in mocking Jesus (27.27–31). They divide His garments amongst themselves (27.35–36), and certainly are aware of the charges against Him.[157] The centurion and his fellow soldiers see the signs surrounding Jesus' death and realize not only His innocence but also His identity: the Son of God. Only Matthew records that the soldiers under the centurion reach the same decision (Mark 15.37; Luke 23.47). Multiple Gentiles realize Jesus' identity as He dies on the cross.

This is an extremely significant moment. The Father has twice declared from heaven that Jesus is his Son (3.17; 17.5). Satan and his demonic companions have identified Jesus in this way (4.3, 6; 8.29). The disciples declare Jesus to be God's Son after witnessing

---

147. Also, see Gillman, "The Wife of Pilate," 162–163 who argued the reason Jesus was not spared because of this dream, like He was in the dreams in Matthew 1–2, was because the warning was ignored by Pilate.

[156] While some argue 2.12 and 27.19 makes no reference to an angel in the dream, neither does Joseph's dream of 2.22. Based on the context of chapters 1–2 and the result of sparing the baby Jesus, it would be odd for the author to record this if he did not see the hand of God in all dreams in the book. For more information on the comparisons and contrast in the dreams see Gillman, "The Wife of Pilate (Matthew 27.19)," 159–164.

[157] Wilkins, *Matthew*, NIV Application Commentary, 907–908.

him walk on water and calm the storm (14.33). When Jesus asks his disciples who they believe him to be, Peter affirms Jesus is God's son (16.16).[158] Up to this point no one outside of God, the demons, and the disciples, has used such language to describe Jesus.[159]

As a matter of fact, the Centurion's confession seems to replace Peter's confession. While all the disciples vow not to forsake Jesus when he goes to the cross (26.35b), Peter was the most vocal (26.33, 35). However, when the time comes, Peter is nowhere to be found and in his place a Gentile confesses Jesus to be the Son of God. The centurion and his companions show greater insight than the disciples. These Roman soldiers acknowledge Jesus' Sonship *in* the cross, not separate from it as the disciples assumed (16.21–22). Additionally, their confession serves as a rejection of the traditional definition of leadership by the Gentiles (20.25).[160] They are learning firsthand what service looks like in God's kingdom, while the disciples are nowhere to be found. Following in the footsteps of the previous centurion encountered in Matthew (8.5–13), these Gentile soldiers possess insights many Jews, including Jesus' own disciples, do not possess.

Judas betrays Jesus (26.14–16, 47–50), Peter denies Him (26.69–75), and the rest of Jesus' male disciples abandon him (26.56). Since women are not viewed as possible revolutionaries (being executed only rarely), as well as being granted more leniency in mourning, it was safer for them to be present at the cross than the other disciples.[161]

Despite these historical circumstances, the author continues to depict Jesus' female followers as more faithful than the male disciples. Ironically, two of the three women are identified by their sons. These women's sons have been selected as disciples by

---

[158] France, *The Gospel of Matthew*, NICNT, 1084–1085.

[159] Ibid, 1085.

[160] Keener, *The Gospel of Matthew*, 687.

[161] Ibid, 689.

Jesus but abandon him while their mothers stay nearby.[162] The author informed the reader these women were not newcomers but had "followed" (Gk. *akoloutheo*) Jesus from the beginning (4.13; 27.55). The word "followed" is used to signify the women were disciples.[163] They began to follow him around the same time he called his first male disciples (4.18–22). They, too, leave everything to follow him,[164] but stay through the cross and to the tomb. Matthew informs the reader that "many" women are present at the cross but does not mention any of the male disciples.[165]

There are multiple connections between the death of Jesus (27.45–56) and the Magi visiting Jesus when he was a small child (2.1–12). The Magi come on the scene, inquiring where they may find the "King of the Jews" (2.3) while on the cross, the sign above Jesus' head reads, "King of the Jews" (27.37). Both contexts present the Jewish Scriptures as being fulfilled (2.6, 15, 18; 27.43, 46). Herod wants to kill the infant Jesus and attempts to gain the Magi's trust to accomplish his murderous intent (2.7–8, 16–18). In the case of the Magi, they are warned in a dream not to report anything to Herod (2.12). Joseph is then warned in a dream by an angel (2.13) about Herod's homicidal plans, which results in Jesus being rescued from the clutches of death (2.14–18). However, all children of Bethlehem under the age of two years old are killed and there is much weeping over the slaughtered children (2.16–18). In Matthew 26–27, the religious leaders follow in the footsteps of Herod and plot to kill Jesus. Pilate's wife has a dream about Jesus and she sends a mes-

---

[162]Sheila E. McGinn, "Why now the Women? Social-Historical Insights on Gender Roles in Matthew 26–28" *Proceedings EGL & MWBS* 17 (1997), 107–114.

[163]France, *The Gospel of Matthew*, NICNT, 1086.

[164]In-Cheol Shin, "Matthew's Designation of the Role of Women as Indirectly Adherent disciples" *Neotestamentica* 41, no. 2 (2007), 399–415.

[165]The gospel of John does seem to depict the Apostle John at the foot of the cross (John 19.25–27).

sage begging Pilate to release this innocent man. This time, the dream is not heeded and Jesus is handed over to the mob to be crucified. Just as the mothers mourned the death of their children, many women weep over Jesus' death (27.55–56, 61; 28.1). Finally, he is buried by one of his disciples, Joseph of Arimathea (27.57–60). However, death does not have the final say since Jesus is resurrected from the dead (28.1–10). Just as the Father sends an angel to warn Joseph about Herod (2.13) so He sends an angel to roll away the stone (28.2)![166]

When Jerusalem hears the reason for the Magi's visit, they are greatly troubled (2.3). The chief priests and scribes know the location where the prophet prophesied the Messiah would be born (2.4–6), but none went to investigate the star or where it would lead them. They have no interest in worshiping the child as the Gentile Magi do! Likewise, on the cross, the crowds mock Jesus and His claims (27.39–44). They ignore the cosmic sign, the earthquake, and the splitting of the temple veil at His death (27.45, 51).[167] However, the centurion and those keeping guard with him cannot ignore these signs but declare Jesus to be the Son of God (27.54).[168] In both accounts there is a heavenly sign tied to a significant event in Jesus' life (star or sky darkened at midday). In both cases, the Gentiles accept it and recognize Jesus' identity while the Jews ignore it.[169]

---

[166] Nguyen, "The Function of the Magi Episode (2.1–12) in the Gospel of Matthew," M.A. Thesis 57–60.

[167] Keener, *The Gospel of Matthew*, 685 explains the Jews could have been reminded of God's plague of darkness which He sent on the Egyptians (Ex 10.21–29).

[168] Nguyen, "The Function of the Magi Episode (2.1–12) in the Gospel of Matthew," M.A. Thesis 57–59.

[169] It should additionally be noted that from a human perspective neither account depicts Jesus as majestic. While babies certainly are cute, they are not kingly and do not inspire great confidence in leadership ability. Certainly, while Jesus was on the cross, having been heavily beaten, with a crown of thrones, and barely able to speak, he hardly struck the

4.28 Matthew 27.57–61

Two women refuse to go home: Mary Magdalene and "the other Mary." They follow Jesus from the very beginning of his ministry (27.55), stand by him at His death (27.55–56), and now, accompany Joseph of Arimathea to the tomb (27.61). Even as Joseph departs from the tomb (27.60), they remain.

Their posture (sitting) is noted only in Matthew. Sitting is the posture of mourning.[170] When Job loses his children and his wealth, he sits to mourn (Job 1.20; 2.8). His three friends fail to recognize him and sit in the dirt with him for seven days without speaking (Job 2.12–13). The prophet Ezekiel sees women sitting and weeping for Tammuz (Ezek 8.14). Tyre and Sidon would have repented, sitting in sackcloth and ashes (Luke 10.13). Several non-biblical sources also describe sitting as a sign of mourning (Homer, *Odyssey*, 5.82; 10.497; Herodotus 1.46; *Helena* 1084; Herodotus, *Histories*, 8.40.1; 8.41.2).[171] While the Synoptics emphasize the women's presence as witnesses (Mark 15.47; Luke 23.55), Matthew is also seeking to present them as mourners. They are faithful women, remaining with Jesus even in death.[172] James and John requested a seat in Jesus' glory (20.20–23), but these women knew a disciple's place was "sitting opposite the tomb." They are willing to share in Jesus' humiliation.[173]

---

pose of royalty. Yet, despite the outward circumstances the Gentiles see with eyes of faith and identify Jesus for who he really is: the Son of God.

[170] Rick Strelan, "To Sit is to Mourn: The Women at the Tomb (Matthew 27.61)," *Colloquium* 31, no. 1 (1999): 31–45. He notes that in John 20.11, Mary Magdalene was standing and weeping. However, in that case she was not weeping for the dead but was weeping because she believed Jesus' body had been moved.

[171] Strelan, "To Sit is to Mourn," 35. He notes this shows the importance of the burial to the Jews and that the burial of Jesus was part of the earliest Christian creed (1 Cor 15.4).

[172] Wilkins, *Matthew*, NIV Application Commentary, 913.

[173] McGinn, "Why now the Women? Social-Historical Insights on Gender Roles in Matthew 26–28," 111.

4.29 Matthew 28.1–10

Mary Magdalene and the other Mary, the same women who sit in mourning outside Jesus tomb (27.61), return to "look at the grave" (28.1). An earthquake occurs, and an angel of the Lord descends to roll away the stone. All gospel accounts record the women as the first witnesses of the empty tomb and the first to receive the news Jesus has risen.[174] The women were the last to depart from Jesus' tomb and the first to find it empty.[175] A woman was the first to understand Jesus' mission went through the cross (26.6–13) and, now, women are the first to hear that Jesus overcame death.[176] The guards are terrified and faint, but the women are able to listen and receive instructions from the angel.[177]

The angel instructs the women to become the first to announce the news of Jesus' resurrection. They are to tell the disciples to meet Jesus in Galilee (28.7). The women hastily depart from the tomb with "great joy" just as the Magi have great joy when they encounter the newborn king (2.10).[178] But instead of encountering a newborn king, the women are the first to meet, see, and touch the resurrected Jesus (28.9). Both the women and the Magi respond the same way: they fall to the ground and worship him (2.11; 28.9). Jesus, just as the angel had done, commissions the women to become the first to share the message of the resurrection. Hilary of Poitiers remarked, "The gender through which death entered the world would also be the first to receive the glory, vision, fruit, and news of the resurrection."[179]

---

[174] France, *The Gospel of Matthew*, NICNT, 1098.

[175] Turner, *Matthew*, BECNT, 675.

[176] Garland, *Reading Matthew*, 268.

[177] Weaver, "'Wherever This Good News is Proclaimed': Women and God in the Gospel of Matthew," *Interpretation,* 400.

[178] Garland, *Reading Matthew*, 268

[179] Simonetti, *Ancient Christian Commentary on Scripture: Matthew 14–28*, 308.

John Chrysostom, another church father,[180] said, "[Jesus] thereby brings honor to women, as I have so often said, honor to that sex which is most prone to be dishonored."[181] The gospel hangs on the resurrection (1 Cor 15.1–19) and Easter hinges on the testimony of women. God entrusted the message of Jesus conquering the grave, with all its implications, to women. God treats everyone, regardless of gender or race, as valuable. Matthew depicts women as proactive agents working courageously to accomplish the work of God and bring glory to His name.[182]

4.30 Matthew 28.11–15

This pericope is unique to the gospel of Matthew. For our purposes we must back up to 27.62–66 to ask if those stationed at the tomb were Roman or Jewish guards. There is no doubt the chief priest approached Pilate requesting a guard to be stationed at the tomb for three days to prevent theft of the body by the disciples. However, Pilate's reply is ambiguous (27.65). The guards first report to the chief priests (28.11) but ultimately seem to be answerable to Pilate (28.14). Does the evidence point toward Jewish or Roman guards at the tomb of Christ?

Pilate's words in 27.65 are ambiguous and could be translated as granting a Roman guard (*have a guard*; see NIV and NLT) or as a comment instructing them to use their own temple guard (*you have a guard*; see NASB, ESV, and CSB). Commentators generally lean toward the fact that the guards were Roman,[183] with a few dissenters.[184]

---

[180]John Chrysostom (AD 344/354–407) was Bishop of Constantinople.

[181]Ibid, 309.

[182]F. S. Spencer. "Women" in *DJG*, 1009.

[183]Wilkins, 944; Keener 696; Turner, 677; Davies and Allison, 655; Lewis, vol. 2, 167.

[184]France, 1094–1095, 1104–1105; Carson, 586; Chumbley, 512.

The general arguments for Roman guards are the Jewish leaders would not have needed to request permission of Pilate to post their own guard. Pilate's ambiguous words are taken as granting permission. Finally, since the guards were hired by the Jews, they would naturally report to them first (28.11) but they were ultimately subject to Pilate (28.14).

Those who argue for Jewish guards see Pilate as fed up with the Jews (see 27.24–26)[185] and take his ambiguous statement as a dismissal of their request. Since the guards report to the chief priests first and there is only a chance that Pilate will hear about this situation, they take those as pointers to the fact the guard was indeed Jewish.

If the guards at the tomb were Jewish, Matthew could be setting up a contrast in the Gentile centurion who guards Jesus on the cross and the Jewish guards who keep watch at his tomb. Both witness an earthquake (27.51, 54; 28.2) and other amazing events (27.51–54; 28.2–4). Both became frightened (27.54; 28.4). Although not witnessed by either guards, resurrection is mentioned in both accounts and testified to by multiple witnesses (27.52–53; 28.5–10).[186] The Gentile centurion witnesses the death of Jesus and the events that surround it and declares him to be the Son of God (27.54). The Jewish guards "witness" the resurrection of Jesus and the events that surround it but accept a bribe to spread a lie (28.12–15). It is the Gentile soldier rather than the Jewish guards who is willing to heed the signs and be honest about what they witnessed.

---

[185] John 19.20–22 could be used to bolster such as claim since Pilate is unwilling to alter what he has written as the charge against Jesus as he hangs on the cross. However, since this piece of information is not included in Matthew, we will not make it a linchpin of our argument.

[186] It is important to remember that the guards at the tomb are not mentioned as seeing Jesus come to life. They felt the earthquake, saw the angel's magnificent appearance, and fainted from fear (28.2–4).

Given the standard way Rome dealt with soldiers who failed their guard duties was to execute them (Acts 12.18–19; 16.27; 27.42),[187] it is odd these guards would freely admit they fell asleep and failed in their mission. One ancient source tells of a guard who failed in his assignment to prevent crucified bodies from being buried and he chose to commit suicide instead of being court martialed and executed (Petron Sat. 112). Normally, Roman soldiers who fell asleep during night watch were beaten, and if they survived, were banished to the shame of their family. In addition to scourging, a guard could be beheaded for such a mistake (Eurip. *Rhesus* 812–819, 825–827). However, in some cases, it was possible to strike a deal and escape execution (Tac. Hist. 5.22). Perhaps this would be such a case where leniency would be shown to the guards.

In the final analysis, it is impossible to be certain about if the guards were Roman or Jewish. Thus, Matthew might not be trying to contrast the Roman centurion who guarded Jesus while he died and the Jewish guards. Regardless, the soldiers at the tomb can be compared and contrasted with the women.

Both are frightened by the sight of the angel (28.4–5, 8), but the guards faint while the women speak with the angel heeding the instructions given (28.5–8). It is not recorded that the guards see Jesus, but the women touch him, talk with him, and worship him (28.9–10). Both leave the tomb in a hurry to carry the message to others: the women faithfully deliver a message of victory and joy to the disciples (28.8, 11) while the soldiers plot to spread lies and deception (28.11–15). Matthew's Passion narrative ends the way it began, women responding appropriately to circumstances while men are pictured as wanting.

---

[187] In Acts 16.27 the centurion there almost commits suicide rather than give an account for the prisoners escaping. Thankfully, Paul is able to prevent him before he harms himself and later that evening, he becomes a Christian.

4.31 Matthew 28.16–20

The fact that the disciples meet Jesus in Galilee shows the women faithfully carry the message to them as they had been instructed. Here, after seeing the resurrected Jesus, the disciples are instructed to share that message with the rest of the world. Both men and women receive the same command in Matthew: share the gospel with others. Jesus speaks twice in Matthew 28, once each to women and men, both times instructing them to share the gospel message with others.

From the very beginning of Matthew's gospel, the author anticipates Jesus being a universal savior. Jesus' ministry begins in "Galilee of the Gentiles" (4.15). Now as he prepares to ascend back to the Father, he commissions His disciples to go to make disciples of the entire world on a mountain located in "Galilee of the Gentiles" (28.16). The disciples' quest to evangelize the world would be assisted by Jesus himself since he would be with them always (28.20). Jesus welcomed all, Jews and Gentiles, men and women, who were willing to be baptized in the name of the Trinity and heed his words.

V

NEGATIVE PICTURES OF GENTILES AND WOMEN IN MATTHEW

One objection a reader of the Gospel of Matthew might raise about the information given above would be that Jesus made negative statements about Gentiles in the book. If the Gospel welcomes the Gentiles then why does Jesus make disparaging remarks about the Gentiles in 5.47; 6.7, 32; 18.17; 20.25? Why record a predominantly Gentile region requesting Jesus to leave in 8.34? Why does Jesus ignore, insult, and only hesitantly heal the Canaanite woman's daughter in 15.21–28?

Another objection along these same lines could be made concerning the inclusion of women. If women are welcomed into Jesus' Kingdom, then why on two occasions are women not among the numbered multitude (14.21; 15.38)? Why does Matthew put James' and John's request to have positions of power off on their mother (20.20–21)?

These references are best addressed by examining them within the context of the book of Matthew rather than in isolation and in supposed contradiction of the larger message of the book.

5.1 Matthew 8.28–34

Jesus comes to the "country of the Gadarenes" (8.28). Given the mention of pigs, which was an unclean animal to the Jew (Lev 11.7), the reader can conclude that Jesus is in a Gentile region.[1]

---

[1] France, *The Gospel of Matthew*, NICNT, 340.

Jesus' "welcoming party" consists of two violent, demon possessed men (8.28). Jesus casts the demons out of the men and allows them to enter the swine, whom they promptly kill. The herdsmen report the events in the city and the city requests Jesus depart from their area (8.33–34). If Gentiles are welcomed, then why depict them as rejecting Jesus?

Nothing within this account undermines the larger theme of Gentile inclusion in Matthew's gospel. Matthew presents many people, both Jewish and Gentile, who reject Jesus and his message. Just a few verses before this account, when people are requesting to follow him, Jesus warns them of the cost of discipleship (8.18–22). Jesus warns the disciples they would be rejected for teaching about him (10.5–42). Jesus is rejected at His hometown of Nazareth even after they witness his miracles (13.54). A young man would not part with His earthly goods and so rejects the teaching of Jesus (19.16–22).[2] Jesus longs to gather Jerusalem, but they are unwilling (23.37–39). To reject Jesus does not mean one is not welcomed (see 22.1–14). One could argue that describing the rejections of both Jews and Gentiles in Matthew's gospel only strengthens the point that Jesus' message was intended for and delivered to all people. Matthew is not idealizing the mission to the Gentiles and picturing every Gentile accepting Jesus while every Jew rejects him. It is only those who hear the message who are able to decide if they will accept or reject it.[3]

Furthermore, Jesus casting out demons shows he is freeing people from slavery to sin and Satan. While Jesus has cast out demons before (4.24; 8.16), this is the first of five specific exorcisms Matthew records (8.28–34; 9.32–33; 12.22; 15.21–28;

[2] Perhaps this is a problem in the current account because they are upset over the loss of their pigs.

[3] This thought was given to me by a longtime friend, Kyle Sanders. Kyle edited my paper and gave me many helpful suggestions. He is not only a good friend, but a fellow laborer in God's vineyard. I thank God for him!

17.14–20).[4] Interestingly, the first takes place in Gentile territory. Jesus will not accept Satan's offer to gain control of the world (4.8–10) but comes to destroy the grip of Satan wherever it is found (Matt 12.25–30; 1 John 3.8).[5]

5.2 Negative uses of "Gentile" in Matthew 5.47; 6.7, 32; 18.17; 20.25

Jesus warns people not to pray (6.7), worry (6.32), or follow the leadership model of the Gentiles (20.25). He said Gentiles love those who love them (5.47) and when someone is disfellowshipped they are to be shunned like a Gentile and tax-collector (18.17). How is the reader to understand the handful of anti-Gentile statements which are scattered throughout the book of Matthew? According to David Sim these verses "affirm that the Gentile world is filled with irreligious people who provide anti-role models and with whom contact should be minimal."[6] Since Matthew included these statements in His gospel it reveals his true attitude about Gentiles.[7]

For Sim to hold this anti-Gentile view of Matthew, he must dismiss the numerous positive examples of Gentiles in the book (discussed above) and the statements of the gospel going to the whole world (24.14), and interpret the great commission to be a mission to Jews alone (28.18–20). He argues that Matthew depicts persecution of Christians by Gentiles, and the community to which Matthew wrote would have experienced much persecution from Gentiles after the fall of Jerusalem.[8] Because of this persecution it is a "fair guess" that "many Jews no doubt remained

---

[4]France, *The Gospel of Matthew*, NICNT, 338.

[5]This is interesting since Jesus opponents accuse him of working with Satan twice (9.34; 12.24)!

[6]David Sim, "The Gospel of Matthew and the Gentiles" *Journal for the Study of the New Testament* 57 (1995), 19–48.

[7]Sim, "The Gospel of Matthew and the Gentiles" *JSNew Testament*, 30.

[8]Ibid, 30–39.

bitter at their treatment by their Gentile neighbors and viewed them with a large measure of resentment and suspicion."[9]

Is Sim right in his evaluation of Matthew being hopelessly anti-Gentile? Is there another or better way to understand these statements?

First, while Sim notes the negative statement about Gentiles in 5.47, he seems to overlook the context in which it was uttered. In 5.43–48 Jesus calls his followers, in contrast to the world's view, to love their enemies and "pray for those who persecute you" (5.44). According to Matthew, persecution will provide an opportunity to share the gospel with the Gentiles (10.18). Paul could say he is in "danger from the Gentiles" (2 Cor 11.26) yet was still willing to preach the gospel to them. Far from causing resentment, persecution forces the disciples to recognize a profound truth: those who do them wrong need the gospel!

Second, we must realize that Jesus makes use of stereotypes of His day to help His hearers understand the points. France argues Matthew is invoking stereotypes not to depict the Gentiles as rejected by God but to present the typical Jewish attitude toward Gentiles.[10] Perhaps one could equate it today with how a preacher might refer to how "the world" behaves rather than how a Christian should conduct themselves.

It is interesting that two of these negative Gentile statements also mention tax collectors (5.46–47; 18.17). Tax collectors and Gentiles love those who love them (5.46–47). When a person refuses to repent from sin they are to be shunned as a tax collector or Gentile (18.17). In the gospel of Matthew, Jesus not only welcomes tax collectors (9.10–11) but calls one to be his disciple: Matthew himself (9.9; 10.3)! If Jesus uses the stereotype of tax collectors to prove a point to his audience but still welcomes them, why could he not do the same with Gentiles?

---

[9] Ibid, 38.

[10] France, *The Gospel of Matthew*, NICNT, 227, 240.

Third, three of these "anti-Gentile" statements appear in the Sermon on the Mount (5.47; 6.7, 32). If, as was suggested earlier, Gentiles are present at this sermon, it is hard to believe Jesus would run them down knowing they were present. However, if he is simply using the term Gentile and tax collector to refer to the world then he is calling all people to forsake the thinking of the world for the ethics of his kingdom.

Fourth, in the context of an "anti-Gentile" statement, Jesus makes a statement which expands his earthly mission. One of Jesus' earthly missions is to save his people (Jews) from their sins (1.21). Later, Jesus states he will die for "many" (20.28; 26.28). Thus, it is not merely the Jews whom Jesus will free from the grip of sin but all people.[11] One of the references to the scope of salvation being widened is in the context of an "anti-Gentile" passage (20.24–28). Perhaps this illustrates Matthew is simply evoking stereotypes his audience understood while in that same context showing the gospel is open to Gentiles.

Fifth, Paul, the apostle to the Gentiles, occasionally makes "anti-Gentile" statements. He rebukes the Corinthian brethren for accepting a type of immorality which the Gentiles would not accept (1 Cor 5.1). He rebukes the Gentiles for worshipping what they do not know or understand (1 Cor 10.19). Paul calls the Ephesian brethren not to walk as Gentiles (Eph 4.17). He bluntly writes that Gentiles are full of lust and do not know God (1 Thess 4.5). If Paul could invoke this type of language to predominantly Gentile audiences surely the readers of Matthew could understand these statements are not promoting the rejection of Gentiles from the Kingdom.

Lastly, Jesus is following in the footsteps of the Jewish prophets who condemn the actions of the Gentiles but hold out hope

---

[11]This thought came to me when I was reading J. Julius Scott Jr, *New Testament Theology: A New Study of the Thematic Structure of the New Testament* (Scotland: Christian Focus Publications Ltd., 2008), 99–103. The way the material was presented gave me this idea.

for their inclusion if they repent. Even though Sodom's "sin was exceedingly grave" (Gen 18.20), God would have spared them for ten righteous people (Gen 18.32–33). The sins of Nineveh "came up before" God (Jonah 1.2), but God, to the disappointment of Jonah, spares the entire city when they repent (Jonah 3.5–4.11). If God spares Nineveh upon repentance, would not God spare a Gentile who needed to learn how to pray (6.7), who is worried about the wrong things (6.32), and who has a wrong view of leadership (20.25)? Jesus' "anti-Gentile" statements are consistent with the Jewish prophets who condemned pagan behaviors, but also extended hope of Gentile repentance and acceptances into the people of God.[12]

5.3 Matthew 10.5–6

After selecting the twelve, Jesus sends them out on the "limited commission." The first instruction Jesus gives them is to preach only to the Jews. "Do not go in the way of the Gentiles, and do not enter any city of the Samaritans; but rather go to the lost sheep of the house of Israel (10.5–6)." Does this passage prevent Jesus' followers from ever taking the gospel to non-Jews?

First, when the context is examined, the reader realizes Jesus anticipates the gospel spreading to the Gentiles. When the disciples will be arrested and put on trial for their teaching about Jesus, they will give testimony to the Gentiles (10.18). The prohibition toward non-Jews is only temporary. Matthew seems to be presenting the same theology that Paul, the apostle to the Gentiles (Acts 9.15; 22.21; Gal 2.9), presents: the gospel goes to the Jew first, then to the Gentile (Rom 1.16–17; see also Acts 13.46).[13] Matthew and Paul's theology is in keeping with the teaching of the Jewish Scrip-

---

[12]Michael F. Bird, *Jesus and the Origins of the Gentile Mission* (New York: T&T Clark International, 2013), 57.

[13]J. Julius Scott Jr., "Gentiles and the Ministry of Jesus: Further Observations on Matt 10.5–6; 15.21–28" *Journal of Evangelical Theological Society* 33 no. 2 (1990), 161–169.

tures and the promises to Abraham (Gen 12.1–3). God promised to bless the world *through* Abraham's descendants, thus the message must go to the Jews first then the Gentiles.

Second, the same Jesus who instructs His disciples to preach to Jews only (10.5–6) later instructs the same disciples (save Judas) to go into all the world (28.18–20). The prohibition against the Gentiles hearing and responding to the gospel is only a temporary restriction. Further, Jesus' willingness to heal Gentiles (8.5–13, 28–34; 15.21–28) not only shows His compassion for them, but ultimately points toward their inclusion (8.10–13).[14]

Third, favoritism does not demand exclusivity.[15] Despite the Jews' bad feelings toward Gentiles, God never intended to exclude them.[16] Israel is God's firstborn (Ex 4.22) and specially chosen people in the earth (Dt 7.6–8). However, God uses Israel to bring other nations to him. The Exodus is to show Egypt that Yahweh alone is God (Ex 7.5; 14.4). God performs signs in Israel to show all nations his greatness (Ex 34.10). He instructs Israel to be a kingdom of priests to the nations and make the nations worshipers of him (Ex 19.4–6). The great commission is a fulfillment of the inclusive ideas presented in the Jewish Scriptures. Jesus, as the fulfillment of the Jewish Scriptures (Matt 5.17–18), gives the great commission.

5.4 Matthew 15.21–28

This passage probably presents the biggest challenge to the inclusive theme. Jesus ignores this woman's original request while the disciples request that Jesus dismiss her entirely (15.23). When she continues to make her entreaty, Jesus again dismisses her by

---

[14]Ibid, 166.

[15]Ibid, 165.

[16]The story of Naaman (2 Kgs 5), Jonah (book of Jonah), and the judgment on the nations (such as Amos 1–2, among other places) shows God's concern for other nations. God giving dreams to Abimelech (Gen 20), Pharaoh (Gen 41), and Nebuchadnezzar (Dan 4) also shows God's concern for all nations.

stating his mission is confined to Israel (15.24). Undeterred, the woman bows down before Jesus and begs for his help. He responds with the insulting slang term "dog" which is how Jews often referred to Gentiles (15.26).[17]

It has been suggested that 15.21–22 contains certain hints that show the reader Jesus will help the woman. First, Jesus is in Tyre and Sidon. Previously, He declares that ancient Tyre and Sidon would have repented if they had seen His miracles (11.20–22). Here is a woman from this very region requesting that Jesus perform a miracle. Secondly, Mark identifies the woman as a Syrophoenician (Mark 7.26) but Matthew describes her as a Canaanite (15.22). Since Canaanite women have already appeared in Jesus' genealogy (1.3, 5), the reader recognizes Jesus would help her.[18] The genealogy connection is strengthened by the fact the woman calls Jesus "son of David" (1.1).

However, this hint of Jesus' willingness to help her does not deal with the negative aspects of Gentile rejection within this story. There are multiple explanations for Jesus' words and actions in this text. Perhaps Jesus' tone of voice or raised eyebrow invites further supplication by this woman.[19] Others have argued Jesus is testing the woman.[20] Still others view this as a cultural struggle. Tyre and Sidon economically took bread away from Israel[21] so Jesus is seeing how the woman feels once the shoe is on the other foot.[22]

---

[17]While there have been attempts to downplay Jesus calling her a dog there is no doubt it is an insult. Wilkins, Matthew, NIV Application Commentary, 539 says, "As a metaphor, 'dogs' is a humiliating label for those apart from, or enemies of, Israel's covenant community (1 Sam 17.43; Ps 22.16; Prov 26.11)."

[18]Keener, *The Gospel of Matthew*, 415 and France, *The Gospel of Matthew*, NICNT, 590 footnote 12.

[19]France, *The Gospel of Matthew*, NICNT, 591.

[20]Wilkins, *Matthew*, NIV Application Commentary, 540.

[21]Garland, *Reading Matthew*, 167.

[22]Blomberg, *Jesus and the Gospels: An Introduction and Survey*, 276.

One idea not often explored is that Jesus is trying to teach the *disciples* rather than the woman. The disciples ask Jesus to send her away because she is annoying them (15.23). When the disciples have sought to send people away in Matthew Jesus rebuked them (14.15; 19.13). As a matter of fact, in 15.1–16.28, the disciples' understanding has been greatly lacking. They fail to understand one of Jesus' parables (15.15–16), and they are slow in understanding his warning about the Pharisees and Sadducees (16.6–12). While Peter makes the great confession (16.13–20), he shows he does not understand Jesus' mission (16.21–23). Finally, the chapter closes with Jesus explaining what discipleship demands (16.24–28). Perhaps Jesus responds this way to expose the disciples' prejudices, show them the woman's faith, and remind them the gospel is inclusive.

There are strong conceptual and linguistic ties between 14.13–36 and 15.21–28 which seem to further our point that Jesus is attempting to teach his disciples a lesson in the way he handles this woman. After the death of John, Jesus withdraws (Gk. *anachoreo*) to escape the crowds (14.13). Yet the crowds followed him and he healed them (14.14). The disciples request that Jesus "send away" (Gk. *apoluo*) the crowds but he refuses (14.15). Instead, Jesus provides the crowds with bread (Gk. *artos*) and fish (14.16–19). Everyone ate, was satisfied, and the leftovers are gathered (14.20). Later that evening the disciples are caught in a storm and as Jesus walks by them on the water, they think he was a ghost causing them to cry out (Gk. *krazo*) in fear (14.26). Jesus assures them by revealing his identity and Peter requests to walk on the water to Jesus (14.28–29). Peter climbs out of the boat and begins to make his way toward Jesus but when he begins to sink, he cries out (Gk. *krazo*) for Jesus to save him (14.30). Jesus does, but chides Peter, and the rest of the apostles, for their lack of faith (14.31). After this amazing display of power the disciples worship (Gk. *proskuneo*) Jesus (14.33).[23]

---

[23] Matthew uses the word *proskuneo* 13 times in the book (2.2, 8, 11; 4.9–10; 8.2; 9.18; 14.33; 15.25; 20.20; 28.9, 17).

After a confrontation with the Pharisees Jesus withdraws (Gk. anachoreo) to Tyre and Sidon (15.21). A Canaanite woman comes to him (15.22) and he heals her daughter (15.28). She cries out (Gk. *krazo*) to Jesus requesting healing for her demon possessed daughter. The disciples tell Jesus to send her away (Gk. *apoluo*) because she is crying out (Gk. *krazo*) and bothering them, but he does not. She approaches Jesus and "bows down before" (Gk. *proskuneo*) him requesting his mercy on her child. While the disciples worship Jesus after witnessing his power over nature, this woman worships before she knows if Jesus will use his power on her behalf. Jesus cites a proverb about giving the children's bread (Gk. *artos*) to the dogs (15.26). She accepts his statement but insists the dogs get the leftovers (15.27). Jesus grants her request and praises her for her great faith (15.28)!

It seems Jesus wants the disciples to learn they should not dismiss anyone who cries out to him. They were certainly worried about Jesus dismissing the Pharisees (15.12), but they did not want to be bothered by an annoying foreigner. Rather than dismiss her, Jesus wants the disciples to imitate and learn from her great faith!

Additionally, the connections between 8.5–13 and 15.21–28 probably highlight the importance of the table and leftovers. In both accounts, a Gentile approaches Jesus with a request to heal someone who is close to them (8.6; 15.22).[24] Their loved one suffers from a severe affliction (8.6; 15.22). Both accounts reference a table (8.11–12; 15.27).[25] Finally, Jesus praises a Gentile for their faith (8.10; 15.28) and grants their request by healing from a distance (8.13; 15.28).

---

[24] France, *The Gospel of Matthew*, NICNT, 589–590.
[25] Turner, *Matthew*, BECNT, 389.

Comparing Matthew 14.13–36 with 15.21–28	
14.13–36	**15.21–28**
After a difficult moment (news of John's death) Jesus to with-draws (14.13)	After a difficult moment (con-frontation with the Pharisees) Jesus withdraws (Gk. *anachoreo*) to Tyre and Sidon (15.21)
Crowds follow and he heals them (14.14)	A Canaanite woman comes to him (15.22) and he heals her daughter (15.28).
Disciples: send away (Gk. *apoluo*) the crowds but he refus-es (14.15)	Disciples: send her away (Gk. *apoluo*; 15.23)
Instead, Jesus provides the crowds with bread (Gk. *artos*) and fish (14.16–19)	Jesus: do not give the children's bread (Gk. *artos*) to the dogs (15.26)
Leftovers are gathered (14.20)	Leftovers for dogs (15.27)
Disciples (14.26) and Peter (14.30) cry out (Gk. *krazo*)	Woman cries out (Gk. *krazo*) to Jesus (15.22–23)
Disciples rebuked for "little faith" and asked why they doubted (14.31)	Woman praised for her great faith (15.28)
Disciples worship (Gk. *pro-skuneo*) Jesus AFTER miracle (14.33)	Woman "bows down before" (Gk. *proskuneo*) Jesus BEFORE the miracle (15.25)

The table language in each account is probably significant. It seems to urge the reader to look backward and forward in Matthew's account. The reader should recall how Jesus uses the table language to speak of the inclusion of the Gentiles (8.11–12). Then, looking forward, the reader sees the next account containing a feeding miracle (15.29–39). As suggested above, it seems the feeding of the 4,000 is not directed to Gentiles but to Jews. Perhaps one significance of this account is not whether the Gentiles are fed, but the fact there are leftovers. The Canaanite woman requests the leftovers that fall from the table (15.27). There are leftovers when the 5,000 are fed (14.20), and the leftover food is gathered in baskets in both events (14.20; 15.37). However, the Greek word used for basket in 15.37 (Gk. *spuris*) is different from the one used in 14.20 (Gk. *kophinos*). The word used in 15.37 (Gk. *spuris*) is the same type of basket that is used in Damascus to lower Paul down from the city wall (Acts 9.25; Gk. *spuris*).[26] Thus, the size of the basket is much greater in the feeding of the 4,000 than the 5,000! Perhaps the point is that while the gospel goes to the Jews first and then the Gentiles, there is adequate "leftovers" available for the Gentiles!

5.5 Matthew 14.21; 15.38

If Matthew shows Jesus welcomes women and children, then why does he fail to include them in the numbering of the 5,000 (14.21) or the 4,000 (15.38)? While Matthew does not attempt to number these two groups, this does not point to them being excluded.

Remember Jesus has used both women (15.21–28; 26.6–13) and children (18.1–6; 19.14) as positive examples for his disciples to imitate throughout Matthew. The disciples attempted to shun the Canaanite woman (15.21–23) and the children that came for Jesus' blessing (19.13), but Jesus accepted both and granted the requests made of him (15.27–28; 19.14–15). Rather than exclude them, Matthew has shown Jesus holds them up as the ideal for which all disciples must strive.

As a matter of fact, these verses point to *inclusion* of women and children rather than *exclusion*. The feeding of the 5,000 is recorded in all four gospels and Matthew is the only gospel

---

[26] France, *The Gospel of Matthew*, NICNT, 603.

which mentions that women and children are present. Mark and Luke simply say 5,000 men are present, with no mention of women or children (Mark 6.44; Luke 9.14), and John does not give a figure or delineation of those present. Only Matthew and Mark record the feeding of the 4,000. While Matthew mentions the presence of women and children (15.38), Mark simply states 4,000 were present (Mark 8.9). Matthew specifies women and are present because he wants to emphasize that they are welcomed by Jesus. They are not only "counted" but are viewed as worthy of imitation.[27]

5.6 Matthew 20.20–23

While Mark records James and John coming to Jesus to request places of honor in His kingdom (Mark 10.35–40), Matthew informs the reader it is their mother who accompanies them and makes the request for them. Is Matthew putting this inappropriate request (it came right after Jesus announces His upcoming death in 20.17–19) off on James and John's mother? Is this woman so blinded by motherhood that she misses the point of who Jesus is and what He has come to do?

First, in Jesus' response, he deals with the brothers as if they are the ones making the request. Then the brothers respond to Jesus' questions (20.22). When the other disciples hear about the brother's petition, they view it as a request made by James and John, not their mother (20.24). Chrysostom warns the reader not to be deceived because Jesus' response shows the brother's request is their own. They convinced their mother to make the request on their behalf.[28] Matthew is not laying the blame for the request at the mother's feet.

---

[27] Sheila E. McGinn, "Why now the Women? Social-Historical Insights on Gender Roles in Matthew 26–28" *Proceedings EGL & MWBS* 17 (1997): 107–114 (107).

[28] Simonetti, *Ancient Christian Commentary on Scripture: Matthew 14–28*, Vol. 1b, 115.

Second, Jesus informs James and John they do not understand their own request. This, in truth, is the request for suffering, not glory. As a matter of fact, the phrase "one on your right and one on your left" only appears in one other place in Matthew: 27.38. In this verse, those on Jesus' right and left are the two robbers who are crucified with Him.[29] The disciples fail to understand how Jesus' path leads to the cross, even though He warns them of this often (20.17–19). While all the disciples forsake Jesus (26.56), there are several women who watch the crucifixion from a distance (27.55–56). Three of these women are specifically mentioned, and it is deeply significant that the final one to appear on the list is the mother of James and John (27.56). James' and John's mother requests her sons be majestically seated on Jesus' right and left (20.20–21), but now she watches as two robbers are crucified on Jesus' right and left.[30] While her sons do not understand their request, she begins to understand what it means to be on the right and left of Jesus. While her sons are nowhere to be found at the cross, she begins to realize what true discipleship is all about. This woman gains the insight her sons sorely need.

---

[29] France, *The Gospel of Matthew*, NICNT, 757.
[30] Turner, *Matthew*, BECNT, 671.

VI

CONCLUSION

While Matthew was probably written to Jews, there is clear evidence the author wanted Gentiles to know the gospel was for them as well. While women were not treated with much respect in the ancient world, Jesus welcomed them into His kingdom. As a matter of fact, these two groups, Gentiles and women, are in some ways held up as the ideal disciple in Matthew. There are two people Jesus praises for their faith: the centurion (8.10–12) and Canaanite woman (15.28). The woman with the flow of blood was healed because of her faith (9.22) and the only specific case of resurrection in Matthew is the synagogue official's daughter (9.25–26). While the disciples do not understand the death of Jesus, a woman anoints him for burial (26.12). While the male disciples forsake Jesus (26.56), the women stand by his cross (27.55–56), mourn at his tomb (27.61), and are the first to be entrusted as witnesses of the resurrection (28.1–10).

The book opens with a genealogy highlighting certain Gentile women, and the faith they show in a variety of circumstances. From the first verses of the New Testament, disciples are called to take the gospel of Christ to all nations and genders. Matthew is truly the gospel for the outcast, especially Gentiles and women. Christianity is truly for everyone. Christianity does not welcome individuals based on ethnicity, gender, status, or wealth.[1] Chris-

---

[1] Michael J. Kruger, *Christianity at the Crossroads: How the Second Century Shaped the Future of the Church* (Downers Grove: IVP Academic, 2018), 12.

tianity spreads so quickly and widely that around AD 150 Justin Martyr could write, "For there is not one single race of men, whether barbarians, or Greeks, or whatever they may be called, nomads, or vagrants, or herdsmen living in tents, among whom prayers and giving of thanks are not offered through the name of the crucified Jesus" (*Dial.* 117).

I feel the need to make a few simple, timeless applications from the information that we have examined above. I pray this brief conclusion helps challenge the reader to become more like Jesus in the way we deal with others.

6.1 No one should be excluded

Perhaps the theme of welcoming the outcast is very personal to Matthew. After all, Matthew is a tax collector. His occupation results in him being rejected by his fellow Jews as a sell out to the Romans. "Tax collector" is often used in connection with, and synonymous with, sinner (Matt 9.10–11; 11.19; Mark 2.15–16; Luke 5.30; 7.34; 15.1–2; 19.1–7). Yet, Jesus welcomes him. Matthew is not the exception, he is the norm with Jesus. Matthew wants everyone, especially the outcasts, to know that Jesus welcomes them.

The question for the modern audience is a simple yet challenging one: are we welcoming the outcasts like Jesus did? Do we judge people by the fact they have tattoos and piercings? If one walks into our worship assemblies with unkempt hair and ragged clothes, do we give them a nod from across the room because we do not want to get too close? How do we respond to the alcoholics or drug addicts that need help getting into rehabilitation facilities in order to turn their life around? The most effective programs in rehabilitating people are faith-based programs.[2] Are we willing to provide that all-important foundation of faith in Jesus Christ in

---

[2] I have no official stats, but this is based off a handful of conversations with police officers and one county judge who, in different conversations, said the same thing.

addition to the counseling and professional help they need? How do we respond when a minority race walks into our assembly? When a family with a handicapped child moves to the area and is looking for a church, are we eager for them to worship with us?

In the first book of the Bible, the author reminds us that men and women were made in the "image of God" (Gen 1.26–27). Paul reminds us men, women, Jew, or Gentile are all one in the Gospel (Gal 3.28). These verses are met with a hearty "Amen!" during sermons and Bible classes and then conveniently ignored when Christians encounter people whose past might be considered "sketchy." Many Christians reason shamefully within themselves: "Why waste our time studying with our neighbor: he/she is an alcoholic/addict/sexual deviant." If a person is incarcerated, they are summarily written off as candidates for the Gospel. Many in Corinth lived immoral, wicked lives that were changed by faith in Jesus Christ (1 Cor 6.9–11). Saul of Tarsus, better known as the apostle Paul, had a horrible past (Acts 26.9–11), but God changed him (Acts 9, 22, 26; Gal 1.13–16). Christians today cannot reject outcasts when the Lord Jesus welcomed them.

Matthew reminds us faith is found in surprising places. A Jew would have never expected for a Gentile centurion or Canaanite woman to have had great faith, yet they do (8.10; 15.28). If the disciples had gotten their way, the Canaanite woman would have been dismissed because she was annoying (15.23). The disciples rebuke the unnamed woman of Matthew 26 for her gracious action toward Jesus. Since faith is found in surprising places, our biases must be put aside, and the gospel shared. Let us faithfully plant and water but leave the growth to God (1 Cor 3.6).

A man rode up on his motorcycle and parked in the church parking lot. He wore a leather jacket and had greasy hair. He looked "rough." He was seated on the back row and many people walked by him without acknowledging his presence. Finally, the preacher walked back, greeted him, and asked what brought him to church that morning. The man responded he was simply looking for someone to study the Bible with him but had been to several churches and no one would talk with him. A study was set up and the man became a Christian. He began to study the Bible, became a great student, and eventually decided to preach the gospel.[3] What if he had been ignored that day on the back pew?

One person told me he hoped a family would start attending our church because they had four young kids. This same person was less than enthused when an older couple became a part of our group. Are we only excited for people to come to Christ when they hold similar or greater social standing than us? Are we only comfortable when those who are in our same tax bracket become Christians but not as excited when the old hermit who lives in the shack on the edge of town is baptized for the remission of his sins? Do we practice the inclusivity of the Gospel that Jesus taught and carried out during His ministry?

6.2 A family in Christ

This concept must be taken one step further. Jesus informs His listeners that those who heed His Father's will are His true family (12.49–50). In Christ, Christians are a family. Paul refers to himself as a father (1 Cor 4.14; 1 Thess 2.11) and mother (1 Thess 2.7) in the faith.[4] New Testament authors often use family language to refer to Christian relationships (Acts 9.17; 1 Cor 6.6; Heb 13.23; James 2.15; 1 Pet 5.12; 1 John 2.9–11; 4.20–21; Rev 1.9).

If our father, mother, sister, or brother had a surgery would we be at the hospital to comfort them? Would we take them food as they recovered? Would we keep their kids for a day to help avoid a daycare bill? Would we call and check on them? Yes! Even if several states (assuming American residence) sepa-

---

[3] This is a true story. The man is a family friend with a godly family.

[4] He also refers to Timothy (1 Cor 4.17; Phil 2.22; 1 Tim 1.2; 2 Tim 1.2) and Onesimus (Philemon 10) as his beloved child.

rate us, we would jump on an airplane to be with them. Are we as eager to serve our family in Christ with the same vigor as we do our natural family?

Do we make excuses about why we are not doing these things? I do not know the Jones family very well, so I am not going to call them. My personality is very different from Brother John's so we will not take food to them. Sister Jane is hard to get along with so I am not going to call and see if she needs her yard mowed. According to Matthew 25.31–46, one issue we will be judged on is whether we have assisted those in the family of Christ. A welcoming, inclusive Christian is a servant to their Christian family in all situations of life.

Jesus shows his disciples there is room in his kingdom for those who come to him in faith. Society might view certain individuals as outcasts, but Jesus looks at their heart and persistence in following him. The women in Jesus' genealogy might first appear to be deeply flawed but serve as great examples of transformation and faith. Jesus pauses not to rebuke the woman with the flow of blood for being in a large crowd, but to praise her for her faith. Jesus' teaching in the Sermon on the Mount and in parables (Matt 13) shows his inclusion of Gentiles and women.

Not only are the "outcasts" welcome but they can serve as examples to replicate. It is the Magi who travel a great distance to give gifts and worship the King of the Jews while Jerusalem is distressed at the news of his arrival. Jesus praises the Roman soldier's faith and holds him up as the ideal for the nation of Israel. Jesus informs the religious leaders they should learn from the example of the people of Nineveh and the Queen of the South who responded appropriately to God's messengers. Jesus applauds the Canaanite woman's faith and calls the disciples to imitate it. The unnamed woman who anoints Jesus' feet before his death is the only person who has grasped his predictions of his upcoming suffering. Thus, Matthew concludes by Jesus instructing his disciples to carry out the great commission. All are welcome and the standard is the same for all (16.24–28). All can serve as positive examples for discipleship of our Lord.

⁞

BIBLIOGRAPHY

Baffes, Melanie S. "Jesus and the Canaanite Woman: A story of Reversal" *Journal of Theta Alpha Kappa* 35 no. 2 (2011): 12–23.

Baughman, Terry R. "Gentile Inclusion in the Kingdom of Heaven as Revealed in Matthew 13." M. A. thesis, Western Seminary, 1999.

Bird, Michael. *Jesus and the Origins of the Gentile Mission.* New York: T&T Clark International, 2006.

Blomberg, Craig L. *Matthew.* The New American Commentary, Vol. 22, Nashville: Broadman Press, 1992.

_____. *Interpreting the Parables.* 2nd ed. Downers Grove: IVP Academic, 2012.

_____. *Jesus and the Gospels: An Introduction and Survey.* Nashville: Broadman Press, 1997.

Brown, J. K. "Gospel of Matthew" Pages 570–584 in *Dictionary of Jesus and the Gospels*, 2nd Edition. Editors Joel B. Green, Jeannine K. Brown, & Nicholas Perrin. Downers Grove: IVP Academic, 2013.

Brown, Raymond E. *The Death of the Messiah, From Gethsemane to the Grave: A Commentary on the Passion Narratives of the Four Gospels*, 2 Vol. New York: Doubleday, 1994.

Capon, Robert Farrar. *The Parables of the Kingdom.* Grand Rapids: Eerdmans Publishing Company, 1985.

Carson, D. A., Douglas J. Moo, and Leon Morris. *An Introduction to the New Testament*. Grand Rapids: Zondervan, 1992.

Carson, D.A. "Matthew" in *The Expositor's Bible Commentary: With the New International Version: Matthew, Mark, and Luke, Vol. 8*. Ed. Frank E. Gaebelein. Grand Rapids: Zondervan Publishing House, 1984.

Carter, Warren. *Households and Discipleship: A Study of Matthew 19–20*. England: JOST Press, 1994.

Chumbley, Kenneth L. *The Gospel of Matthew*. Nashville: Self Published, 1999.

Cousland, J. R. C. "The Feeding of the Four Thousand Gentiles in Matthew? Matthew 15.29–39 as a Test Case." *Novum Testamentum* 41, no.1 (1999): 1–23.

Dickens, Charles. *A Christmas Carol*. New Jersey: Watermill Press, 1980.

Heil, John Paul. "The Narrative Roles of the Women in Matthew's Genealogy." *Biblica* 72, no. 4 (1991): 538–545.

Declaisse-Walford, Nancy, Jacobson, R. A., & Tanner, B. L. *The Book of Psalms*. New International Commentary on the Old Testament. Grand Rapids: William B. Eerdmans Publishing Company, 2014.

Eusebius. *The Church History*. Translation and Commentary by Paul L. Maier. Grand Rapids: Kregel Academic & Professional, 2007.

Eusebius. *Eusebius' Ecclesiastical History: Complete and Unabridged*. Translated by C. F. Cruse. Peabody: Hendrickson Publishers, 1998.

Ferguson, Everett. *Backgrounds of Early Christianity*. 3rd Ed. Grand Rapids: William B. Eerdmans Publishing Co., 2003.

France, R.T. *The Gospel of Matthew*. Grand Rapids: Wm. B. Eerdmans Publishing Co., 2007.

_____. *Matthew: Evangelist & Teacher*. Downers Grove: InterVarsity Press, 1989.

Garland, David E. *Reading Matthew*. Macon: Smyth & Helwys Publishing Inc., 2001.

Gillman, Florence Morgan. "The Wife of Pilate (Matthew 27.19)" *Louvain Studies* 17 (1992): 152–165

Gundry, Robert H. "Book of Matthew" Pages 486–492 in *Dictionary for Theological Interpretation of the Bible*. Editor Kevin J. Vanhoozer. Grand Rapids: Baker Academic, 2005.

Gurtner, Daniel M., Joel Willitts, and Richard A Burridge. *Jesus, Matthew's Gospel and Early Christianity: Studies in Memory of Graham N. Stanton*. New York: Bloomsbury Publishing, 2013.

Greeley, Andrew. *Jesus: A Meditation on His Stories and His Relationships with Women*. New York: Tom Doherty Associates, LLC, 2007.

Hakh, Samuel B. "Women in the Genealogy of Matthew." *Exchange* 43, no. 2 (2014): 109–118.

Hanlon, Daniel J. "The function of the Gentile Characters in the Gospel of Matthew." M.A. Thesis, Trinity Evangelical Divinity School, 2010.

Hayes, J. Daniel. *From Every People and Nation: A Biblical Theology of Race*. Downers Grove: InterVarsity Press, 2003.

Heil, John Paul. "The Narrative Roles of the Women in Matthew's Genealogy." *Biblica* 72, no. 4 (1991): 538–545.

Hertig, Paul. "The Inclusive and Contextualize Mission of Jesus in the Gospel of Matthew" Evangelical Theological Society papers (1999): 1–15. http://legacy.lincolnchristian.edu/library/brary/tren/ETS-0162.pdf

Hutchison, John C. "Women, Gentiles, and the Messianic Mission in Matthew's genealogy." *Bibliotheca Sacra* 158, no. 630 (2001): 152–164.

Iverson, K.R. "Gentiles" Pages 302–309 in *Dictionary of Jesus and the Gospels*, 2nd Edition. Editors Joel B. Green, Jeannine K. Brown, & Nicholas Perrin. Downers Grove: IVP Academic, 2013.

Keener, Craig S. *The Gospel of Matthew: A Socio-Rhetorical Commentary*. Grand Rapids: Wm B. Eerdmans Publishing Company, 2009.

_____. *The IVP Background Commentary: New Testament*. Downers Grove: IVP Academic, 1993.

Kingsbury, Jack Dean. *Matthew as Story*. 2nd ed. Philadelphia: Fortress Press, 1988.

Konradt, Matthias. *Israel, Church, and the Gentiles in the Gospel of Matthew*. Translated by Kathleen Ess. Waco: Baylor University Press, 2014.

Kruger, Michael J. *Christianity at the Crossroads: How the Second Century Shaped the Future of the Church*. Downers Grove: IVP Academic, 2018.

Lea, Thomas D., and David Alan Black. *The New Testament: Its Background and Message*. 2nd Ed. Nashville: B&H Publishing Group, 2003.

Lee, Kukzin. "Jesus and the Gentiles in Matthew." M. A. thesis, Gordon-Conwell Theological Seminary, 1999.

Lewis, Jack P. *The Gospel According to Matthew, Part 1: 1.1–13.52*. Austin: Sweet Publishing Company, 1976.

_____. *The Gospel According to Matthew, Part 2: 13.53–28.20.* Austin: Sweet Publishing Company, 1976.

Licona, Michael R. *Why are there Differences in the Gospels? What we can Learn from Ancient Biography.* Oxford: University Press, 2017.

Love, Stuart L. *Jesus and Marginal Women: The Gospel of Matthew in Social-Scientific Perspective.* Eugene: Cascade Books, 2009.

McGinn, Sheila Elizabeth. "Why Now the Women: Socio-historical Insights on Gender Roles in Matthew 26–28." *Proceedings EGL & MWBS* 17 (1997): 107–114.

Nguyen, Michael Quang. "The Function of the Magi Episode (2.1–12) in the Gospel of Matthew." M. A. Thesis, 2002.

Provan, Iain. *Seriously Dangerous Religion: What the Old Testament says and why it Matters.* Waco, TX: Baylor University Press, 2014.

Reeder, C. "Child, Children" Pages 109–113 in *Dictionary of Jesus and the Gospels,* 2nd Edition. Editors Joel B. Green, Jeannine K. Brown, & Nicholas Perrin (Downers Grove: IVP Academic, 2013)

Roberts, Mark D. *Can we trust the gospels? Investigating the Reliability of Matthew, Mark, Luke, and John.* Wheaton: Crossway Books, 2007.

Scott, J. Julius. Jr. *New Testament Theology: A New Study of the Thematic Structure of the New Testament.* Scotland: Christian Focus Publications Ltd., 2008.

_____. "Gentiles and the Ministry of Jesus: Further Observations on Matt. 10.5–6; 15.21–28." *Journal of Evangelical Theological Society* 33 no. 2 (1990): 161–169.

Shelley, Bruce L. *Church History in Plain Language,* 4th Edition. Edited by R. L. Hatchett. Nashville: Thomas Nelson, 2013.

Shin, In-Cheol. "Matthew's Designation of the Role of Women as Indirectly Adherent Disciples." *Neotestamentica* 41, no. 2 (2007): 399–415.

Sim, David. "The Gospel of Matthew and the Gentiles." *Journal for the Study of the New Testament* 57 (1995): 19–48.

Simonetti, Manlio (Editor). *Ancient Christian Commentary on Scripture: Matthew 1–13*. Downers Grove: InterVarsity Press, 2001.

_____. *Ancient Christian Commentary on Scripture: Matthew 14–28*. Downers Grove: InterVarsity Press, 2002.

Smillie, Gene R. "'Even the Dogs': Gentiles in the Gospel of Matthew." *Journal of Evangelical Theological Society* 45, no. 1 (2002): 73–97.

Spencer, F. S. "Women" Pages 1004–1013 in *Dictionary of Jesus and the Gospels*, 2nd Edition. Editors Joel B. Green, Jeannine K. Brown, & Nicholas Perrin. Downers Grove: IVP Academic, 2013.

Stott, John R. W. *The Message of the Sermon on the Mount*. Downers Grove: InterVarsity Press, 1978.

Strelan, Rick. "To Sit Is to Mourn: The Women at the Tomb (Matthew 27.61)." *Colloquium* 31, no. 1 (1999): 31–45.

Tigay, Jeffrey H. *Deuteronomy*, The JPS Torah Commentary. Philadelphia: The Jewish Publication Society, 1996.

Turner, David L. *Matthew*. The Baker Exegetical Commentary on the New Testament, Grand Rapids: Baker Academic, 2008.

Vitale, Joanna K. "A Comparative Analysis of Depictions of Female Beauty in the Hebrew Bible and the Jewish Apocrypha and Pseudepigrapha." DPhil Thesis, Worcester College at the University of Oxford, 2015.

Weaver, Dorothy Jean. "'Wherever this Good News is Proclaimed': Women and God in Gospel of Matthew." *Interpretation* 64, no 4 (2010): 390–401.

Weren, W. J. C. "The Five Women in Matthew's Genealogy." *The Catholic Biblical Quarterly*, 59 no. 2 (1997): 288–305.

Wilkins, Michael J. *Matthew*. The NIV Application Commentary, Grand Rapids: Zondervan, 2004.

Witherington, Ben III. *Women and the Genesis of Christianity*. New York: Cambridge Press, 1990.

Wong, Richard. "The Gentiles and the Gentiles Mission in the Gospel of Matthew." M. A. thesis, Lincoln Christian Seminary, 1993.

Wongratanamajcha, Suriya. "The Gentiles in Matthew: An Exegesis on the Relationship of the Gentiles and Jesus." M. A. thesis, Lincoln Christian Seminary, 1998.

The Man of Galilee

In *The Man of Galilee,* Haygood argues for the deity of Christ simply from the presentation of Jesus given in the Gospels: Jesus Himself as evidence for His deity. This short book gives a thoughtful, thorough, and logical presentation of the unique and universal quality of the character of Jesus. Preface by Homer Hailey and Ferrell Jenkins. New preface by Dr. Dan Petty.

The Gospel of the Resurrection

In this classic work, B. F. Westcott offers not just a historical defense of the resurrection but also a wide-ranging exploration of the significance of the resurrection for the individual, for the church, for nations, for mankind, and at the widest reach, for creation itself. "The question at issue," he says, "is a view of the whole Universe, of all being and of all life, of man and of the world, and of God." New introduction by Dr. Timothy McGrew.

The Training of the Twelve

One of Jesus' most important endeavors during His short ministry involved the preparation and training of the twelve disciples for the work they would need to accomplish. The importance of studying Jesus' methodologies cannot be overstated. While there is much we can learn from His words and deeds, it is His work in training the disciples that facilitated the promotion and growth of the Kingdom in the first century. If we would become His disciples, we must sit at His feet and be trained by Him as He trained the twelve.

The Mirror or the Mask

Liberating the Gospel from Literary Devices

Lydia McGrew amasses objective evidence that the evangelists are honest, careful reporters who tell it like it is. Meticulous, well-informed, and accessible, *The Mirror or the Mask* is an important addition to the libraries of laymen, pastors, apologists, and scholars who want to know whether the Gospels are reliable.

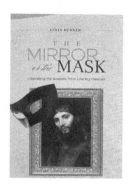

Invitation to a Spiritual Revolution

Studies in the Sermon on the Mount

Few preachers have studied the Sermon on the Mount as intensively or spoken on its contents so frequently and effectively as Paul Earnhart. *Invitation to a Spiritual Revolution* provides an excellent and very readable written analysis which appeared first as a series of articles in *Christianity Magazine*, here offered in one volume so that it can be more easily preserved, circulated, read, reread and made continuously available.

Just Jesus

The Evidence of History

Few people are able to ignore Jesus. He has devotees and detractors, but hardly anyone is neutral about him. But how much do we know about him? Whether we love him or loathe him, it only makes sense that we know what and whom we're talking about. Just Jesus is about what we can know about Jesus. Jesus isn't just a religious idea but a phenomenon of history. That means we can and should ask about him all of the historical questions we can think of and see which ones can and can't be answered. Fortunately, we're able to learn a lot more about Jesus than most people think.